A TOAST

TO THE

TOWN

A history of Beverley's public houses

Paul Gibson

Kingston **Press**

British Library Cataloguing in Publication Data.
A catalogue record for this book is available from the British Library.

First published 2001

Published by Kingston Press

ISBN 1 902039 12 2

Kingston Press is the publishing imprint of Kingston upon Hull City Libraries,
Central Library, Albion Street, Kingston upon Hull, England HU1 3TF
www.hullcc.gov.uk/kingstonpress

Printed by Kingston upon Hull City Council Printing Services,
33 Witham, Kingston upon Hull, England HU9 1DA

This work is dedicated to:

my father
John William Gibson
(1915-1989)

my grandfather
John Gibson
(1881-1963)

my great-grandfather
William Gibson
(1848-1927)

Preface

As I was born in Hull I may owe my interest in Beverley's pubs to my ancestors who were residents of Dunswell. Generally speaking my interest is in all things local to the Hull area, especially pubs, both past and present. I jointly produced an illustrated book on some of the lost pubs of Hull in December 1999 (*Lost Pubs of Hull*, Kingston Press 1999) that is due be followed by a second volume, but I had been investigating Beverley's pubs for some time prior to this.

I found myself wondering about the Sun Inn (no longer the Tap & Spile thank heavens) following a request for some information on its history by the members of C.A.M.R.A. in the summer of 1998. Later, on a purely educational visit - for a quiz as I recall, I began to gather a more personal interest. I had begun to live part of each week in Beverley at the home of my partner Gail and I inevitably started to visit the local hostelries. My previous regular visits had been many years prior to this on nights out with friends around Beverley in the early 1980s (usually on the train from Hull on Friday or Saturday evenings).

The new visits led to a search for all the books and literature on the subject of Beverley's pubs - I was sure that for such an historic town there must be a lot to choose from. Sadly only one small book[1] had attempted to even skim the surface of what I now know to be a very tricky research topic. There had been minor references of more ancient inns in other local books but nothing tangible except Jan Crowther's excellent study "Beverley in Mid Victorian Times", which contained a short summary of Beverley's entertainments during that period. More recently, in November 1998, historian Chris Ketchell had gathered many of these references into a useful chronological listing that he produced as a "*basic framework for any more detailed further study*". My study of the Sun Inn had *set me off* really, and I decided to try and expand a database of the pubs of Beverley that I had begun the previous autumn (meeting Gail had begun my involvement with the computer). It had been an attempt to discover all I could whilst avoiding the pitfalls of it becoming a life's work, which it easily could have done. A sudden change of residence found Gail and I both living in Hull and with the loss of my temporary Beverley passport the project was shelved. Now back in Hull full-time I became heavily involved in the first Hull book and that was that, or so I thought. The Hull book diverted my attention from the tricky subject of Beverley, but not for long.

The Beverley file glared at me from the shelf pricking my conscience until I found the time to give it another shot. Fortunately I do have other topics to work on (and a life) and so this small book is merely the result of a short eighteen months "on and off" study. Most of the work is from mind-numbing, yet dangerously interesting searches in libraries and archives. But it is also the result of discussion with those *in the know* and from my other love, that of collecting old photographs and picture-postcards of Hull and East Yorkshire.

It turns out that Beverley and Hull are quite different in terms of research methods; Hull lost much of its historic architecture in the course of slum-clearance programmes,

---

[1] The Inn Places of Beverley (see bibliography).

blitz damage and subsequent rebuilding, new road schemes and of course changing fashions. During these onslaughts the majority of Hull's ancient inns, taverns, alehouses and beer-houses were lost. Fortunately, Hull is blessed with various well-kept and easily accessible archives of documents, plans and images; the quality of these resources is such that they are the envy of many other cities in the country. Beverley is another matter; its buildings remain for the most part unaltered or affected by war or council policy.[2] Its only worry is its inevitable growth and the damage that over-used lanes and roads, never built to carry the modern levels of traffic, will inevitably bring. Its records and archives so far as they are available, are sadly lacking when compared to Hull. Some unfortunate decisions in the course of changing councils have led to the loss of much archival material. In terms of public houses it is particularly bereft and those records that remain are often only available for reference within the archive offices and have unfortunately not been made available for accurate reproduction in this work. Nevertheless some evidence has come to light in the short time I have studied the subject and I have had limited success in tracing the majority of the "lost" pubs of Beverley as well as having a look at those still in existence.

My hope in publishing this work at a point where I know that there are still some avenues to be explored is that a worthier individual (for worthier read - *someone with more time*) will build upon my initial study and give the subject the full attention it deserves. *Any volunteers?*

Paul Gibson, May 2001

---

[2] A survey of the pubs I have listed reveals that only nineteen have actually been demolished, twenty three other pubs that have closed are still in existence but used for different purposes and thirty-seven are still open for business in 2001.

Acknowledgments

Robert Barnard for support and advice on source material.

Mr. Calvert for permission to copy pictures of the Globe Inn, Pack Horse etc.

Jan & Peter Crowther for discussion regarding the French Horn and the sharing of information and source material.

Pat Elliot for advice on old Beverley maps, plans and news clippins'.

Frank Farnsworth for the use of some postcards.

Chris Ketchell for sharing information, proof reading, debate, discussion and several purely educational visits to the surviving hostelries.

Geoff Percival for information on coins, tokens and pub-checks.

Mrs Pinfold for passing her late husband's notes to a good home.

David Sherwood for newspaper clippins', discussion and his ongoing work on the history and development of Beverley's streets.

Gail Thornton for her patience.

Graham Wilkinson for computer tutorials and friendship.

The staff of the **Hull Local Studies Library.**

The staff of the **Beverley Local Studies Library.**

The staff of the **East Riding of Yorkshire Council Archives and Records Service.**

And everyone else who has assisted in any way, shape or form.

Contents

Introduction

"No, sir: There is nothing which has yet been contrived by man which so much happiness is produced as by a good tavern or inn."
(Samuel Johnson)

The old town centre of Beverley has thankfully remained relatively unchanged for decades and in parts, centuries. This unusual level of preservation has enabled some detailed studies[3] of the town's buildings and their reports make interesting reading. Generally focusing on the architectural beauty of Beverley, by their very nature they offer little in the way of specific studies of groups or building types. Several of Beverley's pubs have achieved amazing longevity and can confidently be dated back centuries in some cases. In terms of variety Beverley has surviving examples of most types of pub building from the simple *beerhouse (e.g. the Blue Bell, Wood Lane)* to the larger coaching inns (*e.g. the former King's Arms, the King's Head, the Green Dragon etc.*). Only the elaborate Gin Palaces are missing from the picture; Beverley as a small town has never had the need of such grand places that were essentially show cases for breweries and confined to the larger cities. The variety is otherwise fairly complete in terms of examples of the different styles of pub architecture. Beverley has only relatively recently bowed to the pressures of commercial demand and allowed some of its historic pub buildings to be modernised. This has usually meant enlarging smaller cosy taps, bars and snugs' into larger impersonal spaces, a

trend it seems that most places of entertainment inevitably have to follow.

Historically the role of the local pub has been much more important than today in the twenty-first century and certainly in the smaller towns such as Beverley. Drinking featured as a part of almost all walks of social life. As well as offering company and comfort for the majority of the visitors to an average alehouse or tavern of the nineteenth century, they had a multitude of other purposes. For those in service they offered a welcome escape from their superiors, they were a meeting place for the young and offered food and shelter for a variety of travellers such as drovers, peddlers and vagrants.

The Beverley skyline from a 1907 picture postcard view. The pubs in view are the Ship Inn Market Place (centre), Globe Inn Ladygate (bottom left) and the original Dog & Duck Ladygate (centre left).

---

[3] Most notably The Royal Commission on Historical Monuments' survey of 1982 and the very useful Pevsner series of guides, the East Yorkshire volume having recently been updated by Dr David Neave.

As the church withdrew from popular entertainment in the sixteenth and seventeenth centuries, family events and rites of passage were often celebrated in the local alehouse. Events such as baptisms, marriages, the *drinkings* that usually followed funeral ceremonies, the end of apprenticeships, and what were known as "bid-ales"- events which raised money for worthy causes or troubled neighbours, were amongst some of the regular events held in the local alehouse or tavern. As well as being the centre for these more personal and traditional recreations they were often used for meetings of the local community and as the centre for markets and fairs.

In Beverley as in other towns the alehouses and taverns developed into what we now know as pubs or public houses, a term derived from public alehouse. The pub gradually became the principal centre for entertainment; skittles, cock-fighting and illegal gambling were common and music and dancing also became more popular, certainly amongst the working classes. Nearer the town's centre they were often used for more varied functions sometimes related to specific trades and wages would often have been paid in the pub (an unhealthy alliance sometimes developed between employers and publicans and wages were often spent before leaving the pub). Meetings of trade associations and friendly societies were often held in purpose built club rooms above or behind pubs and employment was often arranged within the bars.

From the middle of the nineteenth century pubs had to become more attractive to the general public mainly due to the challenge from temperance reformers. The temperance movement offered coffee houses in place of pubs and alternative attractions such as day trips. Pubs had to raise their standards and become more *visible*. It was during this period pubs became more architecturally decorated with illumination playing a large part, often in the form of large lamps hung above entrances inviting the public in. Purpose-built pubs became common and this afforded the owners the opportunity for even grander and more individual decoration leading to the typical pub frontages of the late Victorian era. These alterations often replaced simple Georgian or earlier fronts and Beverley is fortunate to have surviving buildings from both periods.

The number of pubs within Beverley at any one time during its history may have been linked with the rise and fall in prosperity of Beverley's trade and industry. There are some surviving inns from an early period of commercial success when Beverley was an important woollen and cloth centre as well as an important market town (Beverley was the eleventh most populous town in England in 1377).[4] Trading statistics show an early high during the fourteenth century and a gradual decline in the fifteenth century, which was exacerbated by the dissolution of the college in 1548. By the middle of the sixteenth century the wool trade was extinct and trading reduced to weekly markets and annual fairs. However, by 1700 Beverley's trade and prosperity had risen again.

Logically inns and taverns were confined to the main thoroughfares e.g. around the Beck and the routes to and from the markets and the churches. Those buildings that survive from the earlier periods, that were or are now used as public houses therefore are generally situated around Beckside, Flemingate, Highgate, Toll Gavel and the market squares. Sadly very few do remain from the early periods, but notable exceptions are the Sun Inn, the White Horse, and the Lord Nelson amongst others, which as buildings all date from before 1700.

[4] Pevsner.

The majority of Beverley's older surviving pubs (with few exceptions) date from the eighteenth and early nineteenth century, the second rise of its trading and industrial importance.

The number of pubs and this is a very general term that includes alehouses, taverns, inns, beer-houses etc. etc., has remained fairly constant in the more recent past, say during the past two hundred years. Those currently concerned with the alleged rising number of pubs in Beverley should be pleased to know that in 1557 there were thirty-eight drinking establishments in the town and in the year 2000 there were thirty-eight pubs in the town. Despite those highs and lows mentioned earlier, the average number of pubs in the town at any one time during the last four hundred years has rarely been more than forty-four.[5]

The information that follows has been presented in the form of a gazetteer for ease of reference and has been illustrated by the author. I have included maps based on Ordnance Survey plans where appropriate to assist in locating the "lost pubs". I have also re-drawn some floor-plans from originals held in the East Riding of Yorkshire County Archives to give an impression of the changing face of pub design. Beverley it has to be said is pictorially challenged; that is to say I have had little success in finding old images of pubs. What other photographs there are may well be in private collections, and as such unavailable. The pictures that are included therefore are mainly old images from my own collection, supplemented with more modern photographs. All of the modern pictures are by the author unless credited otherwise. There will of course be those people I have been unable to contact who have pictures they would make available and I would ask that if any one has items they think

would be of interest that they contact me through the publisher.

The intention is that the book is used by the reader as a handbook whilst conducting their own research within the pubs, *cheers!*

A scene looking north along Ladygate in the 1920s. To the left, the former Custom House Vaults and to the right the inn-sign of the Globe Inn. Note the complete lack of traffic. (Beverley Local Studies Library)

---

[5] Sample of trade directories etc.

"An Inventory of Ye Goods & Chattels of James Wilson of Beverley - Inn Holder late deceased, taken & valued by those indifferently chosen" October 1686.

Inprimls, Purse & Apparrell	£ 3 : 00 : 00
Items in Ye fore – roome	
1 range with clamps, fire shovill & tongs, 1 large pr. of tongs,	
1 pr. of Racks, a brass chasing dish, iron, pestle & other implements	£ 1 : 00 : 00
In the Little Parlour	
1 Bedstead, Bed & furniture thereof,	£ 2 : 00 : 00
1 truckle-bed with bed furniture & a cupboard & one presse	£ 1 : 13 : 00
In the Great Parlour	
1 Bedstead, Bed & Bedding & furniture	£ 3 : 00 : 00
3 chairs, a long settle, 2 Stools, 1 Presse, 1 Table & a form, 1 table,	
1 range, curtains & rods	£ 1 : 08 : 00
In the Low Parlour	
One bedstead, Bed & Bedding, 1 cupboard, 2 stools,	
tables & other implements	£ 1 : 16 : 00
In the furthest chamber	
1 Bedstead, Bed-curtains & vallans & other furniture. 1 table-cupboard,	
chairs & a stoole	£ 4 : 05 : 00
In the Middle Chamber	
2 Bedsteads & Bedding, 3 tables, 2 forms, 3 stools &	
other implements	£ 1 : 00 : 00
In the 1st Chamber	
2 Bedsteads, 1 bed with furniture, 1 table, 1 form a trunk & cheeses	£ 1 : 10 : 00
In the Brewhouse	
1 copper & Malt salt, Boyler, 3 quart of Malt	£ 10 : 00 : 00
Pewter dishes, flaggons, quarts & port	£ 1 : 06 : 08
In the Buttery	
2 brass-pots, 3 pans, 1 kettle, 2 dripping pans & other implements	£ 1 : 13 : 04
In the Yard	
2 Swyne, Swyne stocks an Helme & other implements	£ 2 : 00 : 00
Hay, Coales & turfes	£ 1 : 00 : 00
Sheets & other Linnen	£ 2 : 06 : 00
Total £ 39 : 18 : 00	

(Reproduced from an abstract supplied by The Borthwick Institute of Historical Research at York University)

An inventory of the items left by a deceased innkeeper of Beverley in 1686. It gives a clear picture of an average inn and its furnishings in the 17th Century.

History and gazetteer

This list is alphabetical and any known pseudonyms have been included as separate entries as well as within the main text for ease of reference. The entries contain a short list of some victuallers known to have been at the pubs taken from a variety of sources, mostly trade directories, census returns and telephone directories. The lists are for interest only and are not intended as a complete list of the tenants of the said pubs. Any victuallers listed in italics are presumed to have been at those premises but no conclusive evidence has yet been found to confirm the link.

Admiral Duncan Inn

Minster Yard South
Also known as the Hallgarth Inn.

Hallgarth Inn was the colloquial name for the Admiral Duncan Inn as its address was Hallgarth, Beverley Parks. Throughout the 19th Century its name changed back and forth in the trade directories as the compilers of the directories interpreted the colloquial names.

The title Admiral Duncan was probably given in honour of the naval hero who defeated the Dutch at Camperdown in 1797 and died in 1804. Shortly after his demise on the 2nd May 1808 Stephen Acklam, an innholder, leased property in *"Lurk Lane Closes- near Flemingate"* from the corporation.[1]
The Hall Garth Inn also had its own brewery. Henry Martin Straker ran the brewery until c1882.[2] Thomas Straker, victualler at the Hall Garth Inn from 1840 until 1870 was also publican of the Black Bull, Lairgate in 1837 and it is probable that this may have been retail premises for the brewery.

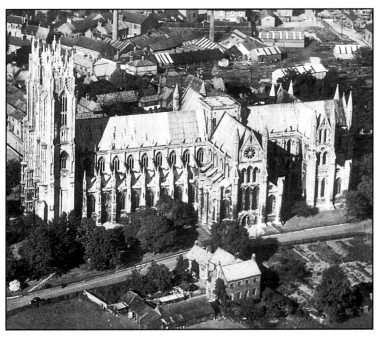

An aerial view of the Minster from the south taken in the mid-1950s. In the foreground are the group of buildings that formed the Hallgarth, including the former Admiral Duncan Inn. Sadly all of the buildings were demolished in 1958.

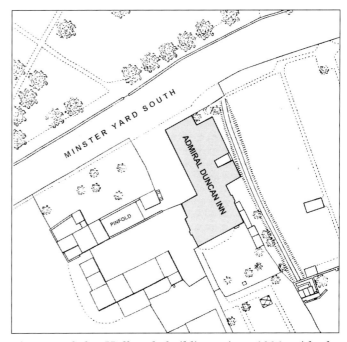

A map of the Hallgarth buildings circa 1890 with the grounds of Beverley Minster to the north.

[1] DDBC/16/350, East Riding of Yorkshire Council Archives.
[2] Hull & East Yorkshire Breweries.

The 1881 Census recorded Henry Straker aged 44, as an innkeeper and brewer resident at the time of the census. Also present were his wife, mother (a *"retired innkeeper"*) one son and three servants. Henry Martin Straker seems to have been an entrepeneur of sorts and is known to have run a theatre in Hallgath in the 1880s that was likely to have been at the inn.[3] In 1896 the Beverley Quarter Sessions made the decision to revoke the licence of the Admiral Duncan Inn as they felt it was *"unnecessary"* in the area. The pub and its brewery were purchased and subsequently closed in 1896 by Canon Nolloth, vicar of Beverley Minster. The buildings including the farmhouse that was still in use, were all demolished in 1958.

Writing of inn-signs in 1939, *The Rambler* noted:

> *"The Hall Garth -The Old Manor House- went out of existence as a hostelry, just over forty years ago. It occupied an unrivalled place in history in the records of 'Beverley's Inns and Houses', for centuries previously. On the outside wall, nearest the Minster, there used to hang a finely executed full-length picture portraying Admiral Duncan, which was the name that carried the licence of this one-time famous inn, inside of which were the remains of a dungeon. The Hall Garth, or Admiral Duncan Inn, was generally looked upon as a Beverley house, but was actually situate in the parish of Beverley Parks."*

A modern property development is now situated to the south of Minster Yard South named Hallgarth Way to commemorate the former buildings.

SELECT VICTUALLERS
1894 R Smelt
1893 George Smelt

1892 R Smelt
1887-89 George Smelt
1877-82 Henry Martin Straker
1840-70 Thomas Straker
1831-34 Robert Crosley
1828-29 Raleigh Page
1826 George Walker
1808-23 Stephen Acklam

Admiral Lord Nelson
Flemingate.
See Lord Nelson.

Albany Hotel
Norwood Dale, Norwood.

"It was agreed by the council in 1896 that the street to the west of the Cattle Market was to be called Norwood Dale".[4] In 1899, soon after Norwood Dale was named the Albany Hotel was listed for the first time in the trade directories; situated at the southern end of a short row of houses which are still in use today.

The Albany may have been named after a racehorse and was one of a small cluster of pubs in or off Norwood that are difficult to separate from one another in the various directories and almanacs. Their names and locations were recorded in very similar ways and Norwood, Norwood Walk and Norwood Dale seem to have been often confused. The pub ceased to be listed in the trade directories after 1926 but was still shown on the Ordnance Survey plan of 1927.

The dealings of the corn exchange were removed from the old exchange in Saturday Market to the former Albany Hotel

---

[3] VCH page 207.
[4] David Sherwood.

8

in 1947, and corn was sold from the site for many years.[5] The building was demolished in the 1950s and the site is now vacant at the north-west end of the Cattle Market yards.

SELECT VICTUALLERS
1899-1926 Robert A Litchfield

Anchor Inn
Beckside.
Also know as the Black Horse.

This property was recorded as an inn as early as May 1st 1809,[6] named the Black Horse, in papers relating to the transfer of the property from one owner to another.

However the property was actually older than this and deeds for the Black Horse/Anchor date from 1745;[7] other references in the documents include:

1st May 1809 - *"Sale to Samuel Bland of... 'piece of waste behind house of S.B. at Beckside known by the sign of the Black Horse...for 3 guineas".*[8]

22nd January 1814 - *"Agreement for sale...for £435...Samuel Bland to William Gray...'The Anchor', formerly the 'Black Horse".*[9]

11th November 1848 – *"Conveyance for £300... 'The Anchor' and a butcher's shop built where the cottage stood".*[10]

4th November 1880 – *"Conveyance for £550...to Joseph Robert Spencer of Beverley, brewer The Anchor and cottage".*[11]

The Black Horse could possibly have been an inn since the earliest date in the deeds (1745) changing its name to the Anchor following the sale of 1814.

The Census of 1851 recorded John Abbott aged 67, his wife and a female house servant present at the Anchor.

Although the Anchor was no doubt a busy pub and one that held a full licence, it was made redundant in 1906 when £1200 was paid in compensation to the owners John Smith's Brewery of Tadcaster. It ceased to be listed after 1906 in the trade directories and in 1907 it was advertised as *"up for sale"* in the Beverley Advertiser.

It was situated opposite the west-end of the beck at the corner of Blucher Lane; the buildings were demolished for road widening circa 1910.

The sign of the Black Horse may have been a reference to a local coat of arms, and although the sign of the anchor has had ecclesiastical links this one was probably a seafaring name. The pub faced the end of the Beverley Beck and was open during the beck's heyday when Beverley earned its title as a port.

SELECT VICTUALLERS
1905-06 Mrs Jessie Spence
1899 John Hancock
1897 Giles Hancock
1892 William Easten
1887-89 John Clark
1882 George H Belliss
1879 William Holt
1872-77 Marr Hill
1870 J Dawson
1867 Samuel Scarr
1864 Josseph Thurlow
1858-59 George Eddon
1855 Boynton Welburn
1826-51 John Abbott
1814-23 William Gray
1809 Samuel Bland

[5] VCH page 221.
[6] Beverley Corporation Minute Book 1707-1835 page 101.
[7] HUMAD ref. DDCV2/3/53.
[8] Ibid. ref. DDCV2/3/73.
[9] Ibid. ref. DDCV2/3/74.
[10] Ibid. ref. DDCV2/3/82.
[11] Ibid. ref. DDCV2/3/84.

A wintry scene looking west in Beckside circa 1905. At the end of the Beck is the Anchor Inn (formerly the Black Horse), which was demolished for the widening of Blucher Lane and other improvements in 1910. (Beverley Local Studies Library)

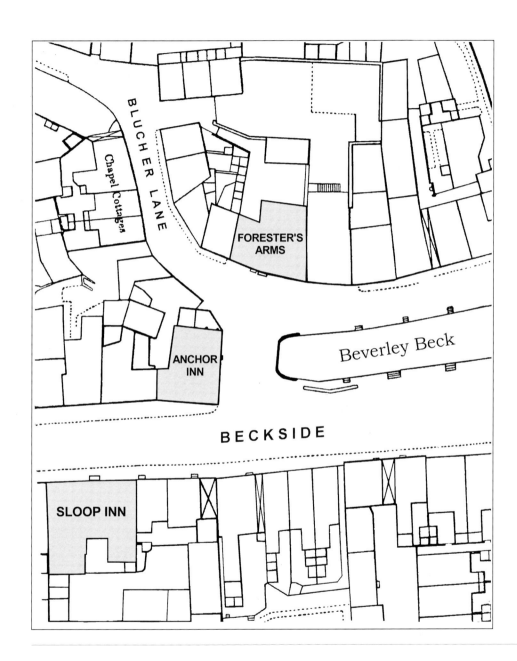

A map of part of the Beckside area circa 1890 showing the former Anchor Inn, the old Foresters Arms and the extant Sloop Inn.

11

Angel
Butcher Row.

The Angel Inn from Butcher Row. The present building is a rebuilt structure that was said to be "recently rebuilt" in 1855. It is now a Grade II listed building.

A rare pub inasmuch as it has retained its original name (as far as we know) for at least 200 years and continues to trade in the year 2001. It is a Grade II listed building[12] and is afforded the limited protection from re-development that this award bestows.

It was known to have been *"frequented by Liberals"* during the 18th and 19th Century.[13] The 1851 Census recorded landlord Daniel Boyes, a famous Liberal, aged 45, his wife, two daughters, four sons, two female house servants, and an occasional nurse (for the children) present at the time of the survey. By the time of the 1881 Census Joseph Garforth aged 62 was licensed victualler at the Angel. He ran the pub with his wife and two apparently very busy servants. One was listed not only as a servant but also as barman and brewer of the pub's ale.

The present building is a rebuilt structure of the mid-19th Century (described as *"recently rebuilt"* in 1855) and it is likely that the original building was a low-building that had been an inn or alehouse for some years prior to its first entry in the trade directories circa 1806.

SELECT VICTUALLERS
1975-87 L J R Arundale
1965 J L Mellors
1955 W L Thompson
1943 A Postill
1939 John Francis Kirby
1929 Adrian Alexander Slesser
1915-21 Louis Spick
1899-1905 Francis Carter
1892-97 Thomas Tempest
1877-89 Joseph Garforth
1846-72 Daniel Boyes
1840 Hannah Arnott
1834 William Arnott
1831-32 John Larcum
1806-29 Robert Larcum

The present inn-sign of the Angel Inn shows a gold coin, originally known as an "angel noble", depicting the archangel Michael slaying the dragon, used from 1465 to the reign of Charles I.

---

[12] DoE serial No.10/18/69.
[13] John Markham.

Arden's Vaults

Hengate.

Francis Alwyn Arden was a wine and spirit merchant who formed his business circa 1786 (although the cellars had been used as wine cellars since at least 1760)[14] with John Barker Arden a surgeon, apothecary and nine times mayor of Beverley.[15] The property was listed as *"Arden's Spirit Vaults"* as early as 1815 in the trade directories.

Arden & Son, wine and spirit merchants and retailers also held an "on-licence" and continued in business until the 1930s; Francis A Arden of No.16 Hengate was still listed as a beer retailer in 1921.

Architectural historian David Neave writing in the revised Pevsner guide said of the building:

> *"...contributes much to the street scene...No.16, Arden's Vaults, of the early 18th Century: two storey with arched doorway to left leading to a brick vaulted cellar 100 feet long and over 20 feet wide [with 7 feet thick walls]. On the front is a stone with the cryptic inscription 'St M's Ch Py' which, like several others in the town denotes St Mary's Church property."*

Arden's Vaults has Grade II listed building status, that was awarded in 1950.[16]

Battle of Trafalgar

Molescroft
See the Molescroft Inn.

Beaver

North Bar Within.
Also known as the Wheatsheaf and the George.

The Beaver has undergone a number of name changes during its life and has also been re-fronted at least once; most recently in mock half-timbering when it was the fashion to do so, probably in the early 1930s.

It was first mentioned in the trade directories around 1790 as the Wheatsheaf, becoming the George circa 1851-53 and the Beaver from circa 1900.[17] The sign of the beaver is most likely a reference to Beverley's coat of arms, which of course contains a beaver.

Wheatsheaf Lane, which runs along the east side of the Beaver was named after the pub and had previously been known as Suggitt's Lane.[18] John Suggitt had been victualler of the pub during the 1820s and 1830s and although the alley was named on a plan of 1841 as Wheatsheaf Lane[19] it continued to be known locally as Suggitt's Lane for many years.[20]

An illustration by W. Megitt of circa 1830[21] shows a signboard with the name John Suggitt hanging from a simple pole outside the pub.

The property would originally have appeared much the same as the adjoining properties within its terrace in North Bar Within. It was altered and given an additional storey sometime before 1861[22] and it is possible that the pub was originally a single property within Wheatsheaf Lane. During the 1850s it was probably extended to include the building fronting North Bar Within. The rear of the property, formerly a kitchen/scullery area is thought to be of 1740-1780 and older than the surviving front buildings.[23]

The census of 1881 listed Headingley born George Bodger, aged 32 as brewer and innkeeper at the inn. Also present were his wife, two daughters and son and one servant listed as an ostler.

---

[14] Jan Crowther. [15] HUMAD ref. DP/16. [16] DoE serial No.9/83/50. [17] Plans for alterations to the George Inn in 1901 referred to the property as "now called the Beaver Inn". BOBE/6, 1901-20. East Riding of Yorkshire Council Archives. [18] David Sherwood. [19] DDX 243/1, East Riding of Yorkshire Council Archives. [20] DDX 24/295, dated 1868. shows the lane as Suggit's Lane. East Riding of Yorkshire Council Archives. [21] Old Beverley illustration No.22. [22] A photograph of 1861 shows the building with three storeys. [23] Royal Commission on Historical Monuments survey.

An image of circa 1860 showing North Bar Within and the original frontage of the Beaver to the left. Then known as the George Inn the victualler is shown as T Smith who was at the pub from around 1855 until at least 1872. (Beverley Local Studies Library)

In 1902[24] it was altered to the plans of Bromet & Thorman of Tadcaster and in 1913 it had a *"new doorway"* added, all work being carried out on behalf of owners John Smith & Co.[25]

SELECT VICTUALLERS
1987 David Barber
1967-75 George Kirby
1929-39 Herbert Higgins
1921 Robert Dunn
1916 Mrs George Bell
1915 George Bell
1905 Miss Jane Ann Wilson
1899 Samuel Grimshaw

The present re-fronted Beaver shown here in 1987 with Wheatsheaf Lane (formerly Suggit's Lane) to the right. (Frank Pinfold)

1892-97 James Haigh
1887-89 Henry Barnes
1882 William R Watson
1879-81 George Bodger
1877 C Greensides
1855-72 Thomas Smith
1846-51 Robert Norriss
1823-40 John Suggit
1806-15 William Dosser
1784-91 William Clark

[24] BOBE/6, 1902-20. East Riding of Yorkshire Council Archives.
[25] BOBE/6, 1913-2. East Riding of Yorkshire Council Archives.

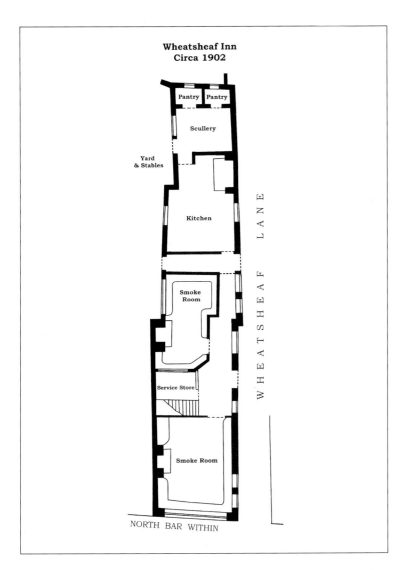

**Wheatsheaf Inn
Circa 1902**

Pantry Pantry

Scullery

Yard
& Stables

Kitchen

WHEATSHEAF LANE

Smoke
Room

Service Store

Smoke Room

NORTH BAR WITHIN

A plan of the Wheatsheaf Inn (now the Beaver) circa 1902 showing the layout of the ground floor rooms at that time. Note the bench seating around both public rooms.

Bee Hive Inn
Keldgate.

The present Bee Hive in Keldgate is not the original building. The original was situated on the west side of Lairgate at No.112. The *new* Beehive situated on the south side of Keldgate, was built in 1957 at a cost of £13,000[26] following the demolition of the original property.

The original property was not shown on Burrow's plan of Beverley in 1747 but is referred to in a bundle of documents *"relating to the Beehive Inn"* of circa 1770, held in the East Riding of Yorkshire Council Archives. They describe amongst other items a *"lease and release"* from John Gale, Edward Brown and Thomas Brown in 1770 to "Jeremiah Brown, innkeeper and wife Anne, of two tenements on the west side of Lare-Gate" (sic).[27]

The census of 1851 recorded William Spenceley aged 56, his wife, one daughter, two sons (one aged 14, an apprentice to a watchmaker), one male servant (a *brewer*) and a general servant. At the south side of the pub was a yard known as Beehive Yard, which is known to have still been residential in 1881.[28]

In 1876 owner Robert Stephenson of the Golden Ball Brewery undertook alterations to the property and it was at this date that a *"new Dram Shop window"* was added (designed by architect William Hawe of Beverley).[29]

The sign of the beehive is a common one and may have been a reference to the trade of an early victualler at the inn or a sign that it was a house for the *workers* of the area! The Beverley Beehive had a marvellous sign in the form of a carved hive.

The last victualler of the old Beehive was William Grant in 1957/58.

[26] Inn Places of Beverley (although plans suggest 1954/55).
[27] DDBC/15/427.

[28] David Sherwood.
[29] BOBE/6, 1876-83. East Riding of Yorkshire Council Archives.

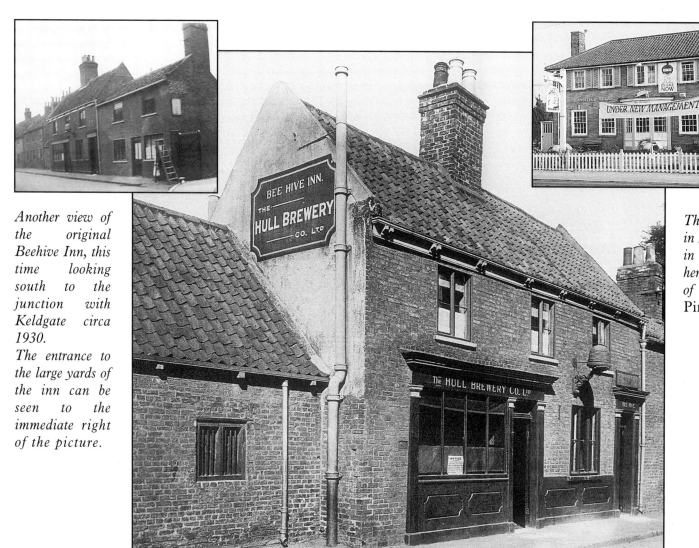

Another view of the original Beehive Inn, this time looking south to the junction with Keldgate circa 1930.

The entrance to the large yards of the inn can be seen to the immediate right of the picture.

The new Beehive in Keldgate, built in 1957, shown here in a picture of 1987. (Frank Pinfold)

The original Beehive Inn on the west side of Lairgate (formerly No.112) shown here looking north around 1925. Note the marvellous carved beehive sign.

SELECT VICTUALLERS
1987 Malcolm Sonley
1975 L J Sharp
1955-65 William Grant
1905-39 Charles Verity
1897-99 George Watts
1892 F.E.Gray
1887-89 William Wilkin
1877-82 Richard Lamb
1869-72 Richard Straker
1867 Edward Stephenson
1864 Ann Spenceley
1832-59 William Spenceley

Beverley Arms Hotel

North Bar Within.
Also known as the Blue Bell.

Little can be added to the history of the Blue Bell written by Beverley historian John Markham in which he described the inn as *"one of Beverley's principal establishments"*, however; An inn known as the *"Bell"* was recorded as early as 1686[30] and was probably the Blue Bell, and the Beverley Corporation Minute Books record that on 18th August 1726 a meeting was held *"at Mr Wellbank's house at the Bell"*.[31] The minute books later recorded *"Robert Norris at the Sign of the Bell"* in 1775 and he was still there in 1772 according to an auction notice of that year.[32]

John Pearson at the Blue Bell Inn, North Bar Street, was the first entry in the trade directories in 1791. The Corporation later gave consent *"to Alderman Middleton, Alderman Arden and Mr Lockwood to extend the fronts of the Blue Bell –'belonging to Messrs Arden and Lockwood'"*- and the house lying between the inn and Crabtree Lane –*'belonging to Alderman Middleton'*. This transaction was dated 7th April 1794 and is probably the date that the Blue Bell was extended to take in other property in the terrace[33] (Crabtree Lane was an older name for Waltham Lane, which adjoined the hotel).

The Blue Bell was re-named as the Beverley Arms Inn in 1794, after these major rebuilding works by local mason William Middleton[34] who is likely to have been the named owner of one of the properties.

In 1804 it was recorded that *"the Corporation has no objection to Mr Greenwood putting out signs in respect of the Beverley Arms"*.[35] The sign in question would have hung from a "gallows style" post stretching out into the road, common in the Georgian period.

A Victorian advertisement for the Beverley Arms Hotel advertising the arrival of new victualler Samuel Fiddes "late of the Black Swan Coney Street York".

[30] VCH.
[31] Beverley Corporation Minute Books page 12.
[32] York Courant 25.8.1772.

[33] Beverley Corporation Minute Books page 77.
[34] John Markham.
[35] Beverley Corporation minute books page 88.

A 1950s picture postcard view of the Beverley Arms pre- 1960s alterations and the addition of the mock coach entrance.

The census of 1851 recorded Samuel Fiddes aged 60, his wife, sister in law, one male house servant, three female house servants, one post boy and one male waiter present at that time.

When the Morley family bought the pub in the 1850s it was noted to have a billiard room, coach houses, a brewhouse, barns and outbuildings, not to mention a large garden that stretched the whole length of Wood Lane. A large paddock at the rear of the garden was used for fetes, travelling circuses and shows. The Beverley Arms was also a Posting Inn or House from the 1840s until the 1890s where horses that pulled waggons or coaches could be hired or changed during long journeys.

The census of 1881 gives an impression of how the inn had grown in terms of business, which was reflected in the numbers of staff resident at the time. Listed were; David Morley Hotel keeper aged 52, born South Cave, his wife, four sons, two daughters, two coachmen, one waiter, one charwoman, one housemaid, one cook, one tea maid, one kitchen maid and one nurse maid.

Trust Houses Ltd. bought the building in 1938 and in 1970 it became part of the Trusthouse Forte group.

Although it had been awarded Grade II listed building status in 1950[36] this had little effect in preventing the major rebuilding that took place in 1966/7. Much of the original property was altered beyond recognition at that point.

SELECT VICTUALLERS
1939 Trust Houses Ltd
1929-37 Benjamin Jagger Dyson
1921 James Arthur Treen

[36] DoE serial No.9/213/50.

1905-16 David Morley
1889-99 Mrs Jane Morley
1867-82 David Morley Junior
1858-64 David Morley
1848-51 Samuel Fiddes
1840-46 John Fiddes
1831-34 Samuel Fiddes
1814-28 Nathaniel Dalby
1784-91 John Pearson
1780 Harry Wilmot
1770 Robert Norris
1726 Mr Wellbank

Black Boy Tavern
Landress Lane

Beverley diarist George Armstrong allegedly recalled the Black Boy as a beerhouse *"kept in a shop at the corner of Landress Lane…now [circa 1917?] a butcher and the Maypole"*.[37] This would suggest it may have been the building at the south side of the Toll Gavel junction; a butcher's and a draper at the time he was allegedly writing.[38]

Black Bull
Lairgate.
See the Tiger.

Black Horse
Beckside.
See the Anchor Inn.

Black Swan
Highgate.
Also known as the New George & Dragon and possibly as the Tiger.

No.25 Highgate was recorded as *"new built"* in 1756 and became the *New* George & Dragon, later the Black Swan, by 1792.[39] There were two George & Dragons in Highgate for a short period but this one soon changed its name from the New George & Dragon to the Black Swan.[40]

Stephenson's Golden Ball Brewery (of Toll Gavel) leased the Black Swan in 1844[41] and by the turn of the century it held a full licence. It ceased to be listed in trade directories after 1908 and was made redundant in 1909 when compensation of £530 was paid to the owner Robert Ranby Stephenson.

David Sherwood noted in his "Lost Streets of Beverley" that *"Thompson's Passage dates back to the 1870s and existed into the 1930s; it was to be found in Highgate"*.[42] Thompson's Passage could have been named after the then victualler of the Black Swan, one William Thompson.

The sign of the Black Swan was a very common one and was used for a variety of reasons e.g. as part of a coat of arms (usually the previous land owner's) but the locals would no doubt have known it as the *"Mucky' Duck"*. It was also noted to have had the common *three tuns* hung from its sign[43] which denoted that wines were also available from within.

The property is another of Beverley's grade II listed buildings[44] and remains intact at Nos. 25 and 25a Highgate, to the south of the Monk's Walk.

SELECT VICTUALLERS
1908 Arthur Smith
1906 George Leonard Sapcote
1905 J Parkin 1892-99 Samuel Bielby
1882-89 William Carr

---

[37] A facsimile of a hand written diary is held in the Beverley Local Studies Library of unknown provenance. It is alleged to have been the work of a Beverley butcher George Robert Armstrong, written circa 1895-1920. It is included here for the sake of completion only. [38] Cook's 1899 trade directory.

[39] Beverley Friary Trust notes. [40] John Wood's plan of 1828 shows two George & Dragons and contemporary trade directories concur. [41] Robert Barnard. [42] David Sherwood. [43] Rambler, see bibliography. [44] DoE serial No.10/91/50.

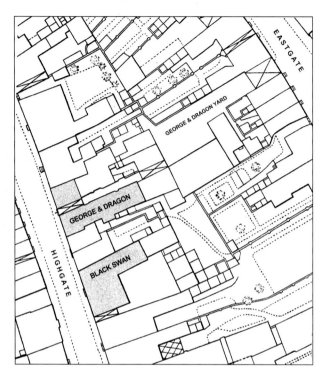

A map showing part of Highgate circa 1890 with its most famous pubs the Black Swan and the George & Dragon (now the Monks Walk).

1877-79 John Turnbull
1867-72 William Thompson
1855-64 John Botterill
1848-51 George Smedley
1846 Thomas Gibson
1840 Hutchinson Stamford
1832-34 John Botterill
1828/9 John Stockdale
1823 Henry Pickering
1791-1815 Nathan Hart

Blue Bell

North Bar Within.
See Beverley Arms.

Blue Bell Inn

Wood Lane.

The Blue Bell Inn was a small beer-house that was scheduled for redundancy in 1909 but was reprieved as it was noted by the licensing committee that:

> *"the landlady is 76 years of age and desires to remain - under the circumstances it might be considered that the license remain for the present".* [45]

It finally closed in the 1940s and the licence was later transferred to a new pub, the Scottish Soldier.[46]
A large blue bell sign was allegedly hung outside the Blue Bell until circa 1920.[47] The marvellous beer-shop window is still in place on the building, which survives on the south side of Wood Lane and is quite rightly a Grade II listed building[48] and is said to be of 1780-1860.[49] The remarkably intact shop window is late Georgian.[50]
On close inspection the west wall of the building reveals that a side door had once existed and to the front the marks where the inn-sign hung are clearly visible.

SELECT VICTUALLERS
1925-39 James Edgar Clayton
1899-1916 Mrs Jane Chapman
1889-97 James Chapman
1879 James Oxtoby/Padgett
1872-77 Joseph Simpson
1864-67 Richard Richardson

---

[45] Beverley Licensing Sessions 31.12.1908.
[46] Inn Places of Beverley.
[47] Rambler, see bibliography.

[48] DoE serial No.9/416/87.
[49] Royal Commission on Historical Monuments survey.
[50] Historic Beverley page 85.

A remarkable survivor, the former Blue Bell beer-house in Wood Lane. The bow window is late Georgian and a Grade II listed building. Shown here in the year 2000.

Blue Boar/Blue Boar & Horns
Toll Gavel.
See Holderness Hotel.

Board
Grovehill.
See Nag's Head.

Board
Ladygate.
See Custom House Vaults / Prince's Feathers.

Boot
North Bar Within.
See Royal Standard / Turf Inn.

Boy and Barrel
Westwood Road.
See Woolpack Inn.

British Workman
Beckside.

Often referred to as a pub but actually a coffee tavern and temperance house, which opened in 1882.[51] The two temperance coffee-houses in Beverley (see also the Market Cross) fought a short-lived battle against the demon drink and are mentioned here for interest only. The British Workman ceased to be listed after 1899.

A 19th Century coin known as a *"refreshment token"* exists for the British Workman and bears the name British Workman Tavern.

[51] VCH page 151.

Buck Inn
Beck Side.

Deeds relating to the property which now houses the Buck Inn date back to at least 1666 however the first reference to it as an inn appears to have been in 1727 when William Smith was listed as the innkeeper.[52]

In 1759 an alehouse licence was granted to Richard Hopwood for "the Buck Inn- *the sign of the Blue Bell*".[53] This curious reference may suggest that the Buck Inn had previously also been known as the Blue Bell and that the signboard or possibly the blue bell itself still hung outside.

The frequent change of tenants at the pub are well documented in archive material held at the Hull University and show that this practice, often thought to be a modern problem where landlords change frequently, is one that has occurred throughout history.

For example:

> 23rd December 1823 – *"Lease and Release for £15...Thomas Pickering of Beverley, labourer and wife Mary (nee Stimson) to Gillyatt Sumner jnr... their share of Buck Inn and adjoining house on N.side of Barley Holme"*.[54]
> 6th April 1825 – *"Lease at £16.4s. rent...Gillyatt Sumner jnr. To Richard Stimson of Beverley, gardener and publican and wife Sarah...Buck Inn and adjoining tenement on E., on N.side of Barley Holme."*[55]
> 6th October 1827 – *"Lease for 7 years at £16.10s. rent...Gillyatt Sumner jnr. To William Bielby jnr. of Beverley, butcher... Buck Inn"*.[56]

The Census of 1851 recorded James Wilkinson aged 57, his wife, two sons and a female general servant all present at the inn on the night of the survey; however some years later the

A sunny day in 2001 showing the Buck Inn on the north side of Beckside. The deceptive front of the pub hides a much older building, possibly of the 17th Century.

following rather sad article appeared in the Beverley Guardian (May 15th 1858):

"SUDDEN DEATH.
It is again our painful duty to have to record another melancholy instance of the uncertainty of human life, in the sudden decease of James Wilkinson, landlord of the

---

[52] DDBC/32/1 onwards, East Riding of Yorkshire Council Archives.
[53] DDBC/32/87 East Riding of Yorkshire Council Archives.
[54] HUMAD ref. DDMC/9/159.
[55] Ibid. ref. DDMC/9/164.
[56] Ibid. ref. DDMC/9/187.

BUCK INN, Beckside. It appeared that on Monday morning the deceased went to work at the Beck, being then in his usual state of health. Between eight and nine o'clock he returned home, and complained of pains and cramp at the stomach. After walking about the yard with the view of obtaining some relief from the intense pain, he went in to the house, and sat down, when his wife asked him if he felt better, but he had only time to imperfectly answer "No," when he instantly expired. An inquest was held at the Sloop Inn on the following day before E.D. Conyers, Esq., Coroner at which Mr. W.W. Boulton, surgeon, stated that he and his father had attended the deceased eighteen months previously, who at that time was suffering from an attack which threatened to bring on apoplexy. He (Mr. Boulton) had not the slightest hesitation in saying that death was caused from disease of the heart. Verdict accordingly." (sic)

In 1878 Henry Wilkinson, son of the late James, carried out alterations to the Buck Inn adding a new kitchen to the rear[57], later owners Worthington & Co. carried out further alterations in 1921.[58]

The Buck Inn has been awarded Grade II listed building status[59] and in its brief description it is described as simply "18th Century", however the deeds of the Buck Inn do appear to date from 1666.

It is clear that the deceptive frontage of the property hides an extremely old core and it is well worth considerable closer investigation.

SELECT VICTUALLERS
1987 John Firth
1965-75 G.A. Hindmarch
1955-56 Mrs D Wilson
1939-46 Herbert Wilson
1929 George Blizzard
1921 Mrs Emily Miriam Scott

1905-16 Walter Scott
1897-99 George H Warcup
1887-92 Mary Elizabeth Wilkinson
1867-82 Henry Wilkinson
1864 Elizabeth Wilkinson
1846-59 James Wilkinson
1840 William Hutton
1834 George Ruddock
1832 William Bielby (jnr)
1828-31 William Bielby
1826 R. Stimson (sic)
1823 Richard Simpson
1814 Thomas Woodmansey
1806 John Simpson
1791 Thomas Woodmansey
1786 William Sumner
1759 Richard Hopwood
1727 William Smith

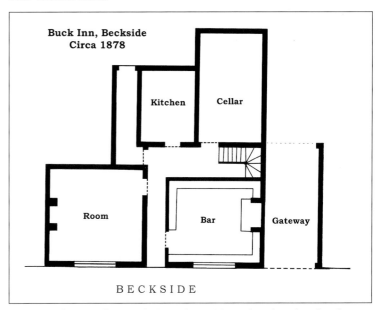

A floor-plan of the Buck Inn circa 1878 showing its simple two room layout with only one "bar".

57 BOBE/6, 1878-146. East Riding of Yorkshire Council Archives.
58 BOBE/6, 1921-8. East Riding of Yorkshire Council Archives.
59 DoE serial No.11/1/87.

Bull

"outside the North Bar."
See Rose & Crown.

Carpenter's Arms

Lairgate.
See Windmill.

Cattle Market Hotel

Cattle Market
See Drover's Arms.

Cherry Tree Tavern

Cherry Tree Lane.

Robert Gibson was listed at a beerhouse in Cherry Tree Lane in White's trade directory of 1867 and was still listed in a trade directory of 1872.

In 1874 William Glossop (of Glossop's Brewery) entered plans for the construction of *"two cottages and a tavern"* in Cherry Tree Lane and this may have been the date of the construction or *rebuilding* of the beer-house known as Cherry Tree House or Tavern. (Architect Robert Clamp of No.20 Scale Lane Hull drew the plans).[60]

William Blakeston, the victualler in 1891, was also listed as a grocer in Grovehill Road from 1881 until 1889. This and evidence from the 1881 census would suggest a corner plot, however the 1874 plans show the new tavern was to have been built on the south west side of Cherry Tree Lane as a detached building, nearer the railway lines. It is possible that

the stores and the tavern were separate buildings, both simply simply using a popular colloquial name. Further detailed research is required although it is possible that the building at the corner of Cherry Tree Lane was an early beer-house and that a later one existed within Cherry Tree Lane itself. "Cherry Tree House" was still listed as a beerhouse in Ward's Almanac of 1893, however it had also been listed several times as an off-licence and is likely to have been both. The "Cherry Tree Stores" continued to be listed as an off-licence into the 1940s.

SELECT VICTUALLERS
1915 A E Hardy Junior
1905-12 A E Hardy off licence
1892-99 Thomas Altham Jackson, beer retailer & grocer
1881-91 Wm Blakeston
1867-72 Robert Gibson

Cock & Bottle

Beckside.
See Forester's Arms.

Cornerhouse

Norwood.
Also known as the Furlong & Firkin, the Valiant Soldier and the Holderness Tavern.

The Corner House opened for business late in 1999 and had previously been re-named the Furlong & Firkin in 1996. These modern and possibly ill-advised name changes required alterations to what is one of Beverley's finest old pubs despite its Grade II listed building status.[61] Its listed

---

[60] BOBE/6/23- 1874, East Riding of Yorkshire Council Archives.
[61] DoE serial No.9/284/87.

building description suggests that it is of the 18th Century and possibly with even older origins.

Records of rentals paid to a John Courtenay during the period 1796-1806 included rent paid for the *'The Valiant Soldier'* in Norwood.[62]

Another record regarding the property, of 21st August 1811 noted:

> *"an agreement for the purchase from Mr Courtney by Mr Lockwood, of the house called 'the Valiant Soldier' at Norwood corner for £450, and the agreement made with John Botterill, the tenant thereof, for pulling down part of the house. The surveyors to view the property and direct the taking down of part of the house necessary for widening the road from Walkergate and Hengate into Norwood, and the building up of the walls against the part of the house remaining".[63]*

Walkergate had previously been a long winding lane with a narrow opening into Norwood at the junction of Hengate. It is obvious that the narrow entry was causing a problem for carts and carriages and the documents suggest that it was slightly widened around this date.

Another document of 4th September 1811 recorded:

> *"So much of 'The Valiant Soldier' at Norwood Corner as is not required for the widening the street to be sold to Mr Beverley and Mr Duesbury for £250. Being the value assessed according to an estimate made by John Prattman, joiner and Thomas Dalton, bricklayer, Beverley – and undertaking to build up the 'Gavel' end next the ground where part of the premises was taken for widening the street".[64]*

The Cornerhouse, formerly the Furlong & Firkin, the Holderness Inn and more familiarly the Valiant Soldier as shown here in 1987. The building was originally symmetrical and lost its western end for the widening of Walkergate. (Frank Pinfold)

Later, in the 20th Century the junction was widened further due to the increased levels of traffic in modern Beverley; an attempt to ease the traffic in the centre of the town.

The Census of 1851 recorded the splendidly named Phineas Musgrave victualler aged 44, his wife, three daughters, three sons, a niece, one female house servant, a nephew, a brother in law and a brother present on the evening of the census.

By the 1881 census the equally large family of John Griffin were resident. With him were his wife, three sons and three daughters.

Internally the Valiant Soldier has been altered regularly from 1927 onwards (Linsley & Co.).[65]

[62] HUMAD ref. DX/60/6.
[63] Ibid. page 106/7.
[64] Ibid. page 107.

[65] BOBE/6, 1927-18. East Riding of Yorkshire Council Archives.

Writing in 1939, *Rambler, an old-time Scribe*[66], noted:

"The old sign of the Valiant Soldier, well portrayed, was removed some thirty or forty years ago [circa 1900]. This, it is pleasing to note, has to some extent been replaced by an illuminated lantern sign, on either side of which is depicted a warrior mounted on a prancing steed. This recent revival is commendable, at night, when the light displays the sign to advantage, the idea proves very effective."

Sadly that internally illuminated sign is now also gone and the pub has no sign at all other than a large letter C. Despite having been renamed several times in recent years it continues to receive local awards and the continued approval of its regulars.

SELECT VICTUALLERS
1987 Ronald Thewlis
1955-75 F J Simons
1943 William Mann
1937-39 W P Hutchinson
1929 Laurids Madson Lauridson
1921 Herbert Gladstone Lowther
1915-16 William Alfred Cawkill
1905 Edwin James Andrews
1899 Caleb Hornsey
1892-97 Edwin Ellis
1887-89 Susannah Garham
1881-82 Phineas Musgrave
1879-81 John C Griffin
1877 C Kitchin
1848-72 Phineas Musgrave
1846 William Hutton★
1840 Daniel Boyes
1832-34 William Heward
1826-28 Thomas Dunn
1823 John Botterill

1814 William Ackrill
1811 John Botterill
★Although recorded in the directory in 1846 Mr Hutton died in 1845 (Hull Advertiser 5.9.1845).

Cross Keys Hotel
Lairgate.

A fine building of the mid-1760s[67], which enjoys Grade II *star* listed building status[68] and is situated on the west side of Lairgate opposite Old Waste, with Cross Keys Yard to its south.

The York Courant newspaper[69] ran an advertisement in November 1770 that read:

"TO BE SOLD
Almost Opposite the Market Cross in Beverley;
LOT 2; A well built brick and tyled Malt Kiln, with stables for six horses, stable yard, Dog kennel and yard; and the reversion in Fee of a well accustomed Inn or Public House, known by the sign of the Cross Keys, expectant upon the death of a person aged 70, with the stabling and garth belonging thereto. The whole being freehold and convenient situate for the market. Inquire Mr Bowman, the owner".(sic)

The 1791 trade directory recorded that Beverley coaches ran from Hull to *"Mr John Smith's Cross Keys Inn, Back Street"* (an earlier name for Lairgate).
Documents in the East Riding of Yorkshire Council Archives show that the Cross Keys, Lairgate was sold for £1000 in October 1809, to John Simpson of Beverley innholder, by Richard Simpson innkeeper, of Leconfield.[70]

---

[66] See bibliography.
[67] Pevsner.
[68] DoE serial No.9/148/50.

[69] Hull Local Studies Library.
[70] DDBC/31/903.

It was again advertised *"to let"* in the Hull Advertiser of 17th October 1823 and *"for sale"* in the Hull Advertiser of 25th May 1832.

In the census of 1851 George Green aged 51, his wife, nephew (a watchmaker), two female house servants, a *"boots"* and a visitor were all present at the Cross Keys.

The Beverley Guardian ran an auction notice in 1889 that gives a clear impression of the inn at that time. A commercial room, a bar, a smoke room and the usual domestic quarters occupied the ground floor, with cellars below. A sitting or dining room, four bedrooms and (a very modern amenity) a bathroom were on the first floor, with another seven bedrooms, the servants bedroom and a box room on the floor above. Outside there was stabling for 20 horses and the owner rented adjoining accommodation for another 30.

The interior still retains fine details worthy of its Grade II *star* listing including an excellent early 18th Century staircase.

An advertisement for the Cross Keys Hotel from circa 1900 when William Whitehead was the victualler.

SELECT VICTUALLERS
1987 Dennis Armstrong
1975 H Brown
1967 Stanley W Massey
1955 Roy Francis
1939 W Simms
1937 Stanley Walker
1929 James Alfred Sharpley
1921 Isabella J. Millett
1912-16 Henry Millett
1899-1905 William Whitehead
1897 Anna Margaret Keighley
1892 C Keighley
1882-89 Henry Newlove
1877-79 Frederick Ward
1864-72 George Ward
1834-59 George Green
1828-31 William Sissons
1826 Peter Killin 1823 William Clayton
1809-15 John Simpson
1791 John Smith
1784 William Sissison
1770 Mr Bowman

Custom House Vaults
Ladgate.
Also known as the Board / Prince's Feathers.

The Custom House Vaults was originally known simply as the Board circa 1828 and was soon renamed the Prince's Feathers. As another *Prince of Wales* beerhouse had opened in Eastgate this property appears to have been re-named the Custom House Vaults circa 1834 to avoid any confusion.

In 1834 Henry Johnson had begun brewing at his Ladgate Brewery and the pub was the *"tap"* of the brewery and maltings complex to which it was attached. It was noted on a plan of 1868 as the "Retail Vaults Shop" of the Ladgate Brewery's Maltings (*Mr H Johnson's property*).[71]

[71] Robert Barnard.

Robert Attwood Litchfield owned the Custom House Vaults, the Albany Hotel and the Litchfield Hotel from circa 1899. He also had the hairdresser's premises at No.32 Toll Gavel, next to his Litchfield Hotel and ran the Oberon Hotel in Hull in the 1890s.

In 1885 Johnson's carried out alterations to the spirit vaults and it is likely that at that time the *shop* took on the appearance it has today.[72]

It was made redundant as a fully licensed pub in 1909 when compensation of £835 was paid to the owner R. A Litchfield. The pub building and many of the other brewery buildings also survive. The pub building is situated at the corner of Sow Hill and Ladygate and is a Grade II listed building[73] of the 18th Century latterly used as a Red-Cross shop.

The former Custom House Vaults at the corner of Ladygate and Sow-Hill taken in 2001. The "pub" was the retail vaults shop of Johnson's Ladygate Brewery of which many original buildings survive in this area.

Custom House Vaults, Ladygate Circa 1885

SOW HILL

Office

Passage

Counter

Dram Shop

Tap Room

Passage

LADYGATE

A floor-plan of the Custom House Vaults of circa 1885. How cosy must it have been in the snug with the open fire.

SELECT VICTUALLERS
1899-1910 Robert Attwood Litchfield
1893-97 John Agate   1889 Johnson & Co
1887 Frances Johnson
1867 Robert Smelt
1858-64 Samuel Smelt
1848-51 William Lovell
1846 Cristopher Wilson
1840 Robert Clark
1831-34 William Adamson
1828/29 James Wardell

Dog & Duck Inn
Ladygate.

The present Dog & Duck Inn situated at the south-east corner of Dog & Duck Lane is a rebuilt structure, which has replaced a much older inn. The *new* Dog & Duck was built for John Smith's Brewery in the summer of 1929.[74]

---

[72] BOBE/6, 1885-152. East Riding of Yorkshire Council Archives.
[73] DoE serial No.9/315/69.
[74] BOBE/6, 1929-9a *"New public house"*. East Riding of Yorkshire Council Archives.

Documents in the East Riding of Yorkshire Council Archives regarding land transactions in Dog & Duck Lane dated 1822/23 refer to Dog & Duck Lane as *"alias Burden Midding Lane"* and *"now called Dog & Duck Lane"*.[75] This shows how the name of the lane had gradually changed to that of the inn at its corner, obviously well established by that date.

In 1745 Robert Burton, innholder of the Fox in the Dings leased a *"parcel of ground used as a common midden place at the south east end of Ladygate"*. This was possibly the date the original Dog & Duck was built, however the Victoria County History states that Dog & Duck Lane had been known as such since 1799.[76]

The Census of 1851 recorded William Green aged 60, his wife, two sons (one a painter & gilder), an ostler and two female house servants present on the evening of the survey. This shows the inn must have had stabling, as an ostler was someone who took care of horses at an inn.

The Dog & Duck's inn sign at one time reputedly, showed a duck swimming with a dog looking enviously on and with the duck in the dog's mouth on the reverse side.[77] The *sport* of 'Dog & Duck' was a cruel game which involved setting dogs on a duck with tied wings in a river or pond and was more likely to be found at a pub near a village pond or a local stream, e.g. the Dog & Duck at Walkington. The sport was one of many forms of gambling to be found at inns and taverns during the 18th Century. This may be seen as another indication of the first pub's age as a watercourse had previously run at the rear of the inn in Walkergate.

Dog and Duck Inn,

LADYGATE, BEVERLEY.

CHARLES LORD - - - **Proprietor.**

**Good Smoking and Singing Rooms.
Wines and Spirits of the Choicest Brands.
Sparkling Ales, Stout, & Aerated Waters.**

*GOOD STABLING, LOOSE BOXES, EVERY CON-
VENIENCE FOR CARRIERS & TRAVELLERS.*

Cyclists specially catered for.

National Telephone 600.

An 1899 advertisement for the old Dog & Duck. Note "good smoking and singing rooms" were offered.

SELECT VICTUALLERS
1975-87 David E McCullen
1965-67 Harry Webster
1937-55 Fred Middleton
1921-29 Horatio Thomas Holmes
1915-16 Mrs Agnes Andrews
1899-1905 Charles Lord
1882-97 Mrs Sarah Green
1867-79 Thomas Green
1858-64 John Henry Larcum
1834-55 William Green
1831 Hugh Hanes
1823-29 George Sheffield
1814/15 Richard Hopper
1806 Thomas Hobson
1784-91 Edward Hobson

---

[75] DDBC/31/529 onwards.
[76] Page 171.
[77] George Dickinson, writing in the Beverley Advertiser.

Drovers Arms
Corporation Road
Also known as the Cattle Market Hotel.

There were no buildings shown on this site on the 1852 Ordnance Survey plan of Beverley, however, there appears to have been two Cattle Market Inns at the end of the 19th Century and it is extremely difficult to distinguish one from the other in the trade directories. There was confusion in the directories between Norwood Walk, Norwood Dale etc. (the 1910 Ordnance Survey Plan showed Cattle Market Lane as

The Cattle Market Tavern shown here in 1987 was later to become the Drovers Arms. It currently stands derelict awaiting demolition. (Frank Pinfold)

Norwood Walk) and the Drovers/Cattle Market could have been interpreted as having been situated at the bottom of Norwood Dale. In actual fact it was in the next lane known colloquially as Cattle Market Lane. Cattle Market Lane appears to have been first mentioned in the 1881 census and kept this name until 1937 when it became Corporation Road.[78]

The current building is a re-built structure, probably of the 1940s but may have been rebuilt at the time Corporation Road was developed.

A drover was/is someone who drives cattle to market and this pub was originally called the Cattle Market. The building is most likely a 1930s rebuild of an earlier building and is situated opposite the gates of the cattle market. Latterly known as the Drover's Arms, it closed in 1999 and is currently derelict and awaiting demolition.

SELECT VICTUALLERS
1987 Robert Colgrave
1975 B Thorley
1965-67 Alan Fox
1929-55 Walter Gray
1926 Frank Gray
1915-16 Charles Wm Brown (Market Hotel)
1912 William W Acred (Market Hotel)
1905 John Cole
1897-99 Susannah Todd (Norwood Dale)
1894 J Lawson
1892-93 Thomas Ralph Musgrave
1889 Mrs Susannah Gardham
1879-87 Thomas Ralph Botterill
1877 T White (Market Hotel)
1872 James Steel
1867 Joseph Ramshaw
1858-64 Henry Wilkinson

---

[78] David Sherwood.

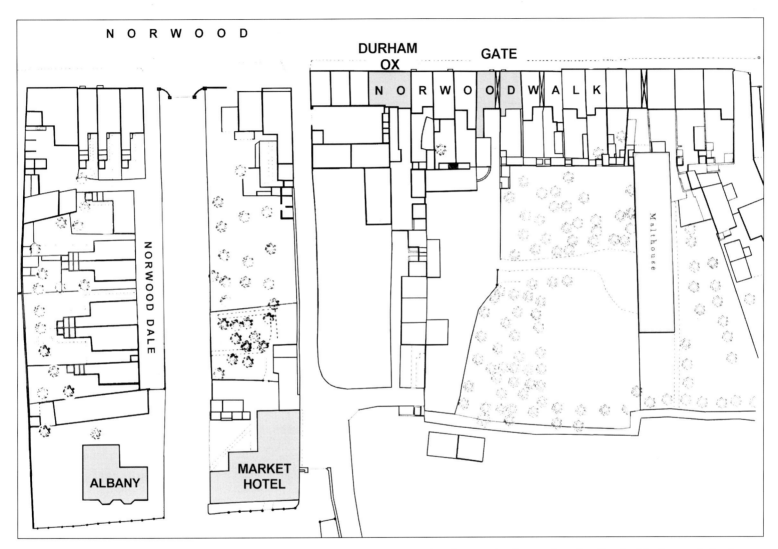

NORWOOD

DURHAM OX GATE

NORWOOD WALK

NORWOOD DALE

Malthouse

ALBANY

MARKET HOTEL

A map of part of Norwood showing Norwood Walk circa 1890. Note the cluster of pubs serving the Cattle Market and the former malt-house of Henry Johnson at the rear of Norwood Walk.

Duke of York
Keldgate.

A plan of Beverley in 1747 by William Burrow showed a small parcel of land on the south-west side of Keldgate in the ownership of a Mr. Meek. There was later a Robert Meek, who was listed as an innkeeper in the 1784 trade directory, however, the first confirmed victualler of the Duke of York was William Akester. A shoemaker by trade, he was recorded in a trade directory of 1814/15.

William Akester was shown to have occupied land owned by the council on a plan of 1806 within *"Beverley Parks"*. In total it was just over 4 acres, for which he paid 15 shillings a year in rent.

Records in the East Riding of Yorkshire Council Archives show that in 1815 he leased a *"close on the north side of Shepherd Lane in Beverley Parks"*, and was listed in that document as an innkeeper.[79]

Shepherd Lane ran off the east side of what is now Queensgate and to the south of Acacia House in Keldgate. George Armstrong allegedly remembered *"the Duke of York was pulled down about 1906"* and the land used for the enlargement of James Taylor's house. James Taylor was listed at Acacia House Keldgate in a 1905 trade directory. Acacia House survives today at the south-east side of Keldgate almost at the junction with Queensgate. It appears to have had an addition to its original structure, to its east and this is likely to have been the site of the Duke of York.

Of Acacia House, George Armstrong allegedly recalled:

"...This house (Acacia) was built in 1837 by William Farrah grandfather of the present Samuel Farrah. Miss Farrah married a man of the name Westerby and she left land at her death to support the free dwellings at the end of Keldgate next to Queensgate Road. The pump opposite Acacia House is still known to some as Fox's Pump".[80]

Make of this what you will, although Mr Armstrong's recollections are as yet without provenance there is no doubt that the Duke of York existed.

SELECT VICTUALLERS
1834 Richard Skinner
1814 -31 William Akester

Durham Ox
Norwood.
Also known as the Ox.

The Durham Ox was one of many pubs to have taken its name from an almost legendary gigantic Ox bred in Durham circa 1800.

In 1881 Francis Wilson aged 34 was recorded as a beerhouse keeper and bricklayer at the Durham Ox with his wife and son.

The present building appears relatively modern but beneath its exterior is a much older building possibly of the 18th Century. It is in effect all that remains of a long terrace fronting Norwood called Norwood Walk.[81] The line of its roof, which shows two different levels on either side of the chimney stack, suggests it had originally been a single property within the terrace and expanded at some date. It was scheduled for redundancy as a beerhouse in 1909 but the decision was not upheld and it carried on trading.

Following the demolition of the three houses to its west during the development of Corporation Road in 1937 it became a corner property, which it remains today with some late 20th Century alterations.

79 DDBC/16/387.
80 Page 70-71.
81 Shown on 1853 Ordnance Survey Plan.

1987 Dennis Hall
1965-75 J L Parker
1955 E Ambler
1943 C Pinder
1936-39 Harry Soames
1929-30 Arthur Beal
1925-27 Florence Coates
1921 George William Coates
1915 William Henry Driffield
1913 F Carter
1909 Annie Hewson
1908 George West
1905-06 T. Woodmansey
1899 Jeremiah Carr
1892-97 William Wilkin
1881-89 Francis Wilson
1874-77 R Bruce
1864-72 John Raspin
1855 Caroline Johnson
1848-51 Robert Moore
1846 Elizabeth Roxby
1831-40 Richard Roxby

The Eager Beaver in Highfield Road, originally known as the Scottish Soldier. Shown here in 2000 with what is one of Beverley's best pub-signs.

Eager Beaver

Highfield Road.
Also known as the Scottish Soldier.

This pub was originally called the Scottish Soldier and was built in the Model Farm Estate in 1966 and can be seen as a fair example of pub architecture at that time. It took its licence from the old Blue Bell in Wood Lane. It was renamed the Eager Beaver circa 1986.

The sign of the Eager Beaver is a reference to Beverley's coat of arms in the same manner as the Beaver in North Bar Within. The present signboard of the Eager Beaver is one of the finest of Beverley's modern pub signs although it is now showing signs of wear.

East Yorkshire

Victoria Road.
Also known as Friar Tuck's.

This huge new pub opened as the East Yorkshire circa 1994 to serve the inhabitants of one of Beverley's new housing developments and was recently known as Friar Tuck's for a short while. Following a fire and temporary closure in November 2000 it re-opened and continues to trade successfully as the East Yorkshire once more.

This pub is as good an example as any of what will no doubt become known as 1990s pub architecture.

Fleece Inn

Beckside.
Also known as the Golden Fleece.

It is known that the road from Beverley to Hull was one of the first to be turnpiked by the turnpike trustees in 1744. The turnpike began at *"the Golden Fleece Inn in Beckside"*.[82] The inn was mentioned again in the Beverley Corporation Minute Books of 21st April 1755 when *"the road from the Golden Fleece to the crane [is] to be levelled for paving, and two keel loads of sea gravel to be sent for the purpose"*.[83] The inn itself had probably stood for many years prior to this as its name was an allusion to the woollen industry which had been a staple trade for Beverley during the Middle Ages.

By the time of the 1881 census only the innkeeper, 43 years old Elizabeth Marson was resident at the inn with one boarder. The beck had seen its heyday come and go and there were many other pubs in the area to serve the trade. The Fleece Inn held a full licence but was made redundant in 1906 when £500 was paid in compensation to the owner Robert Ranby Stephenson.

One of the roadside walls of the Fleece still survives in part and some of the old window openings etc. of the pub can be seen at the rear. The obvious age of the brickwork still visible and the ancient name of the inn confirm that it was probably one of Beverley's oldest.

SELECT VICTUALLERS
1905-06 William Alfred Bielby
1899 J W Gray
1897 Joseph Peters
1887-93 John Backhouse
1881-82 Mrs Elizabeth Marson
1864-79 James Garbutt Marson
1864 Eliza Suddaby
1858-59 James Bishop
1840-55 John Harrison

1831-34 William Harrison
1823-29 Sarah Elstob
1814/15 Sarah Stemeson (sic)
1806 George Stephenson
1791 William Kirkhouse

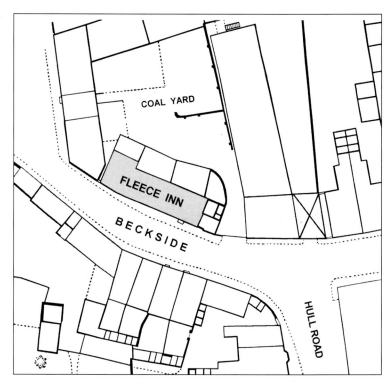

A map of part of Beckside circa 1890 showing the site of the Fleece Inn, which closed in 1906. The southern wall of the building survives in part and although rendered some windows and doors can be made out from the rear.

---

[82] VCH page168.
[83] Beverley Corporation Minute Books page 35.

34

The old Foresters Arms, formerly the Cock & Bottle shown here in a photograph of circa 1925. These buildings were demolished for the present Foresters Arms in 1938.

Foresters Arms

Beckside.
Also known as the Cock & Bottle.

A deed dated 28th February 1792 mentions a *"lease for a year - Elizabeth Oxtoby & James Edmond to Richard Judson - messuage now used as a public house, four adjoining tenements and a large garth on north side of Beverley Beck"*.[84] This may suggest that the messuage (a term used in deed to signify a dwelling house and the surrounding property) had then only recently opened as a pub and indeed its first record in the Poll Book was in 1784.

John Dove a later victualler, was also the brewer of Ladygate Brewery circa 1817-1834.[85]

A possible reason for the first name of the pub the Cock & Bottle, was that it held cockfights, a very popular *sport* until

The present Foresters Arms shown here in 2001. A typical example of the mock Tudor or half-timbered design that was popular in the late twenties and the thirties.

[84] HUMAD ref. DDMC/9/107
[85] Robert Barnard.

finally being prohibited by law in 1849. Coincidentally, it was around that date the Cock & Bottle changed its name to the Foresters Arms.

Beverley's various lodges of the Foresters Friendly Society were founded between 1839 and 1844 and may well have met here, thus accounting for the new name.

The Census of 1851 recorded Thomas Scarr aged 43, his wife, one stepson, two daughters and four sons at the Foresters Arms.

The pub was altered in May 1900 for owner Robert Stephenson of the Golden Ball Brewery[86] but the current property is a completely rebuilt structure of 1938[87] in typical *roadhouse* style similar to others in Beverley of the same period e.g. the Rose & Crown and the Tiger. Some nice features remain around the doors including an illuminated sign above the entrance lobby and some carved stonework within the mock-Tudor hood-moulds of the door surrounds. Sadly one of the original matching pair of entrances has been bricked up at some point.

SELECT VICTUALLERS
1987 Tony Parker
1967-75 J A Mee
1965 A E Johnson
1915-55 Arthur Henry Carlisle
1905 E.H.Butt
1897-99 Walter Scott
1892 A Grogan
1889 Mrs Jane Gibson
1887 John Henry Gibson
1882 E Loft 1879 Levi Lunn
1877 T Porter
1872 Mrs Sarah Scarr
1869-70 T Scarr
1864 Samuel Bielby

1848-59 Thomas Scarr
1840-46 Timothy Loft
1832-34 William Dennison
1826-29 Martha Dove
1784-1823 John Dove

Fox
Dings

What is thought to be a 17th Century pub token or *check* exists with the legend *"At the Fox in Beverley"* with the initials of the victualler –WS- and those of his wife I or J on the reverse. This small coin may provide some evidence of the age of the Fox but provides no evidence to its location. However on 1st April 1734 the corporation leased a *"messuage in the Dings to Robert Burton innholder"*.[88] Later, on 15th November 1784 they granted *"Leave to Robert Burton, surgeon to project a bow window at his house in the Dings late known by the sign of the Fox"*.[89]

On 7th December 1772 the council granted a *"Licence to Robert Wood butcher, to assign a house in the Dings known as the Sign of the Fox to Thomas Brown Junior butcher for 21 years"*.[90]

The last known record of the Fox was on 23rd August 1805 when a *"Lease and Release for £245 was granted from Thomas Fox of Cottingham, gentleman to Richard Empson junior of Beverley, a glazier… all that messuage and shop formerly used as a public house"*.[91]

The latter reference to Mr Fox gives a possible reason for the name of the pub, which is now another of the Dings' lost pub sites and one can only imagine the array of signs and carvings that hung from this short row of property. Is it possible that the Fox was one of the existing properties within the Butter Dings, the Push Inn for example?

---

[86] BOBE/6, 1900-7. East Riding of Yorkshire Council Archives.
[87] BOBE/6, 1938-27. East Riding of Yorkshire Council Archives.
[88] DDBC/16/127, East Riding of Yorkshire Council Archives.
[89] Beverley Corporation Minute Books 1707-1835.
[90] Ibid. page 66.
[91] HUMAD ref. DDCV/15/364.

Freemasons Arms

Ladygate.

The property that was once partly occupied by the Freemasons Arms still exists on the east side of Ladygate being Nos.3 to 5 near the corner of Hengate, opposite the old Johnson's Brewery.

The Census of 1851 recorded Thomas Duffill aged 35, his wife, one daughter and a female house servant all present at the Freemasons Arms. Sadly the Hull Advertiser reported in January 1853 – *"landlord's wife robbed and thrown from train"* and was accompanied by a colourful article that described Mrs Duffill's unfortunate experience.

The following advertisement appeared in the Beverley Guardian August 25th 1860:

> *"TO LET, the DWELLING-HOUSE and SHOP, situate in Toll Gavel, late in the occupation of Mr. Flower, butcher. Also, The FREEMASONS ARMS situate in Lady Gate. Immediate Possession will be given, and further particulars may be obtained on application to W.R. LUNDIE."* (sic)

The property that once housed the Freemasons Arms had originally been one four-bay house of the late 17th Century, which became divided in two late in the 18th Century. A document in the Hull University Manuscripts and Archives Database (HUMAD) dated February 1684, records property being leased to Mary Fox of Beverley; a *"messuage and maltkiln on the west side of – and two messuages on the east side of –Ladygate"*. This may be an early reference to the site of the Freemasons' Arms.[92]

The Freemasons Arms occupied the northern half of the property (No.3) and was recorded as a *pub* from circa 1848 until circa 1867. It was shown clearly marked by name on the Ordnance Survey Plan of 1853. A former victualler, Thomas Duffill was recorded as a retired innkeeper in the 1881 census at No.1 Duffill's Yard, Eastgate.

After a chequered life the building was saved from ruin in the late 1970s and returned to its former single-property status. It is difficult to picture the property as a pub but it may have had some relation to the brewery complex that was to its immediate south and also directly opposite. The building is a Grade II *star* listed property in which it is described as of the *"late 17th Century"* with the front being *"of the late 18th Century"*.[93] A postcard image of the property from circa 1905 shows the building still with its two doorways.

SELECT VICTUALLERS
1858-67 Joseph Wilkinson
1848-55 Thomas Duffill

A picture postcard view of Ladygate looking south from the junction with Hengate circa 1905. On the immediate left is the building that was once partly occupied by the Freemasons Arms. It has since been converted back to one house and hides a late 17th Century core.

(Frank Farnsworth)

[92] DDCV/15/49.
[93] DoE serial No.9/126/50.

French Horn
Highgate.

The only records available for this long-lost pub are a collection of deeds in the East Riding of Yorkshire Council Archives and in the Hull University Archives, amongst which are the following references:

25th November 1802 – *"Final Concord for £260: Peter Denton gentleman, plaintiff...4 messuages, stable, curtilage (court) and garden in parish of St.Martin's"*.[94]
8th January 1807 - *"French Horn in Highgate, occupied by Peter Denton"*.[95]
9th April 1807 - *"The French Horn in Wednesday Market to be let"*.[96]
21st September 1807 - *"Robert Smith carpenter of Beverley granted a lease of the; 'French Horn' in Londoners Street [an early name for Highgate] for 6 years at £322 p.a. plus 8% on money laid out in repairs of stables and outbuildings"*.[97]
2nd May 1808 - *"Thomas Arnott, innkeeper leased "the French Horn on the west side of Londoner Street"*.[98]
3rd February 1823 - *"The former building known as the French Horn Inn was leased to Robert Arnott for 10 years from Old Lady Day 1823 for a rent of £12 p.a. on condition that he "repair the same premises in a substantial and workmanlike manner" within two years and leave it in the same good state of repair at the end of the lease"*.[99]

The French Horn is thought by several local historians to have been the present café at the north-east corner of Highgate; the south side of Wednesday Market. However, the reference from 1808 above listed it clearly as being on the west side of Highgate. In earlier documentation repairs were required of the owner to stables and outbuildings and a garth or garden and a court were mentioned. It is difficult to see how all of the buildings and gardens would have fitted into the rear of the present café property. To the west however, the property fitted the description well, with cart access and gardens. A reference in the trade directory of 1791, which lists it in Wednesday Market would seem to suggest that it was at the very north end of Highgate.

There is still room for debate on its location however, as John Wood's plan of Beverley made in 1828 showed gardens to the rear of the properties on both sides of Highgate.

There was a Talbot Inn in Highgate during the 17th Century[100] the location of which is unknown but it is possible that the French Horn may have been the same property.

If it was the corner café then beneath its aged exterior is an even older core of pre- 1690.[101]

SELECT VICTUALLERS
1808-1820? Thomas Arnott
1791-1807 Peter Denton
1784 Peter Denton Jnr.

French Horn
Ladygate

A single reference in the 1861 census suggests there was a beerhouse known as the French Horn (also possibly the Greyhound[102]) at the northern corner of Ladygate and Dog & Duck Lane, opposite the Dog & Duck Inn. The victualler was Samuel Smelt and the beerhouse may only have existed for a short time.

By the census of 1871 a licensed lodging house was listed on the site, which remained as the *"Model Lodging House"* for many years.

[94] HUMAD ref. DDCV/15/191.
[95] Beverley Corporation Minute Books 1707-1835 page 94.
[96] Ibid. page 95. [97] Ibid. page 96.
[98] DDBC/16/351, East Riding of Yorkshire Council Archives.
[99] P A Crowther. [100] VCH.
[101] Royal Commission on Historic Monuments survey.
[102] The *Rambler* (see bibliography) lists the Greyhound in Ladygate briefly.

Furlong & Firkin
Norwood
See the Corner House.

Friar Tuck's
Victoria Road
See the East Yorkshire

Garibaldi Inn
Flemingate.

In May 1862 the Beverley Guardian recorded that *"a private in the Militia was charged with creating a disturbance at the Garibaldi Inn in Flemingate"*.[103] Further references to this beerhouse are few and it never appeared by name in the known trade directories.

An article in the Beverley Guardian in 1863 regarding the celebrations for the marriage of the Prince of Wales and Princess Alexandra of Denmark reported on the flags etc. that were hung from every shop:

> *"Some of them bearing rather curious inscriptions, as an instance of which we might mention are belonging to a tannery, suspended from the Garibaldi Inn, Fleming-gate upon which was inscribed, "Nothing like leather".*

It is also known that Hull artist John Widdas painted the inn sign of the *Old* Garibaldi Inn, Beverley.[104]
Writing of Beverley's inn signs in 1939, The *Rambler* wrote:

> *"The Garibaldi, which was situate just over the railway crossing, in Flemingate, on the right-hand proceeding in the direction of Beckside and was a well-known licensed house in the seventies and eighties"*.[105]

George Armstrong allegedly noted *"Garibaldi beer house on south side of old Coup en Kell. J Roxby, tenant"*. Old Coup en Kell was a reference to Copenkeld Lane, which ran off the north side of Flemingate near the railway lines. This would have made the pub either No.26 or 28 Flemingate both now sadly demolished.
Garibaldi was probably one of England's first *superstars* or media celebrities. He visited England in 1864 and caused quite a stir wherever he spoke. It is almost certain that this pub was named in his honour, possibly after a visit to Beverley. It is likely however that the beerhouse was in existence prior to his visit.

SELECT VICTUALLERS
1872-77 Mary Marson
1867 Wm Marson
1864 Mark Bell
1858-59 Wm Morrell

Gate Inn
Norwood.

The Gate was another beerhouse in Norwood that proved difficult to place *"on the ground"*. Its inn sign was described by *The Rambler* in 1939 as:

> *"The Gate, four-barred, in Norwood, was opposite the present grounds of the Girls' High School, and was noticeable for the following doggerel lines thereon: - This Gate hangs well and hinders none, Refresh and pay and travel on"*.[106]

---

[103] Beverley in Mid-Victorian Times page 71.
[104] Hull Times 8.10.1904.
[105] Rambler, see bibliography

The census of 1881 recorded long-term (at least fourty years) victualler William Harper as a beerhouse keeper and cowkeeper aged 77 with his daughter (housekeeper), one son in law and a grandson resident at the Gate.

The Beverley licensing sessions considered the licenses of the Gate Inn and the Durham Ox, both in Norwood, in 1909 and both were allowed to remain open. Moors' & Robson's brewery immediately carried out improvements to the facilities including the construction of a *"urinal and new privvies"*.[107] The Gate was finally made redundant in 1914 when £500 compensation was paid to the owners Moors' & Robson's Ltd of Hull.

It is almost certain that the Gate was the beerhouse recorded at the former No.56 Norwood, part of the terrace now almost totally demolished known as Norwood Walk. The only remnant of Norwood Walk is the Durham Ox at No.48 and the Gate was to its east. A 1965 photograph shows the former Gate as the largest building in the block.

The remainder of the site of Norwood Walk is a now marked by a line of modern flats although the First World War Roll of Honour for the men of Norwood Walk has been re-sited at the eastern end of the new buildings.

This circa 1965 photograph of Norwood Walk shows the Durham Ox on the right and the site of the former Gate Inn. The Gate Inn is clearly visible as the large building in the centre of the picture with an arched central passage. (Hull Local Studies Library ©Hull Daily Mail)

[106] Ibid.
[107] BOBE/6/1909-19. East Riding of Yorkshire Council Archives.

George

Highgate.
See the Monks Walk.

George

North Bar Within.
See the Beaver.

George & Dragon

Highgate.
See the Monks Walk.

Globe Inn

Ladygate.

The updated edition of the Pevsner guide describes the Globe Inn as *"of the 17th/18th Century, demolished 1960s"*.
One of the earliest recorded victuallers at the Globe Inn was Daniel Newton at the *"sign of the Globe"* in 1772.

He was recorded in an auction notice in the York Courant newspaper of 11th August 1772.

A bundle of deeds relating to the Globe Inn in the East Riding of Yorkshire Council Archives note that *"a lease for £400 was granted in January 1777 from Ann Nelson spinster, of Beverley to William Artley late of Hornsea now of Beverley innholder"*. The lease was for *"The Globe Inn with garth, garden, stables and cockpit in Ladygate"*.[108] Ann *Nelson* could have been the widow of David Newton and her surname misread in the deeds.

Globe Inn Yard was situated behind the pub (entered through an arch from Ladygate) and at one time contained many small houses. The yard, owned by the landlord, was used for the Beverley Pig Market during the middle of the 19th Century[109],[110] as well as the aforementioned cockpit where locals would no doubt have gambled on the cock-fights.

Visiting shows and touring groups of players including Bostock & Wombwell's Circus stabled many animals in the Globe Inn Yard on their visits to Beverley.[111] John Wood's plan of Beverley in 1828 showed land to the rear of the Globe belonging to Mr Larcum whose family held the inn circa 1826-1840.

The Census of 1851 recorded Francis Dale aged 54, his wife, three daughters, one son, a waiter, a female house servant and a lodger at the inn. In the Hull Advertiser of 24th March 1854 the Globe was noted for sale:

"All that well accustomed and old established inn site; the brewhouse &c stables and every requisite for conducting a large business late in the occupation of Mr. Francis Dales. Also a piece of ground used for the Beverley Pig market immediately adjoining to and laid open with the yard of the inn..." (sic)

[108] DDBC/15/257.
[109] Jan Crowther.
[110] VCH page 222.
[111] Beverley Advertiser 30.4.1999.

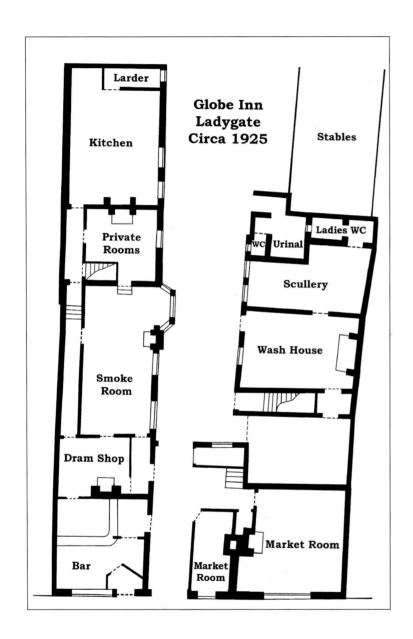

**Globe Inn
Ladygate
Circa 1925**

Larder

Kitchen

Stables

Private
Rooms

Ladies WC

WC | Urinal

Scullery

Wash House

Smoke
Room

Dram Shop

Market Room

Bar

Market
Room

A floor plan of the Globe Inn circa 1925, which shows the extent of its many rooms. Note the "Market Rooms" at the south (or Ladygate) end of the property.

A rare photograph of the Globe Inn Ladygate from circa 1930. The bar is clearly visible to the right of the building, as is the central entry into Globe Yard. All of the buildings were lost when Sow Hill was extended to Walkergate in 1968 - a great loss. (Beverley Local Studies Library)

The census of 1881 listed Thomas Thirsk as licensed victualler aged only 25 with his wife of 24, a son, daughter and two female domestic servants at the inn.

John Smith's Brewery carried out major *improvements* to the Globe Inn during 1925 to the designs of Bertram Wilson a Tadcaster surveyor and architect.[112] The plans show that although the Globe property covered a large area the actual drinking areas covered only a small part of the site, to the left of the arch into Globe Yard. The *"Market Rooms"* covered a larger area and were presumably where pigs and other livestock were bought and sold.

Sadly the pub was closed in 1963 and demolished in 1968 to create a link between Sow Hill and Walkergate. New housing in Globe Court and Globe Mews off Sow Hill Road now occupies the site. The demolition of the Globe although seen as unavoidable at the time, was a very sad loss for Beverley's heritage not to mention its pub architecture.

A fortunate survivor from the demolition was a glazed door, which is preserved in the kitchen of a Keldgate house.[113]

SELECT VICTUALLERS
1929-56 James Cass
1897-1921 David Collinson
1892 Mrs A Ombler
1881-89 Thomas James Thirsk
1872-79 Thomas W Dunning
1867-70 George Smelt
1864 Richard Sugden
1858-59 John Smith
1846-55 Francis Dales
1840 Alice Larcum
1826-34 Thomas Larcum
1823 Alice Wilson
1777-1815 William Artley
1772 David Newton

Golden Ball
Toll Gavel.

Robert Stephenson bought the Golden Ball pub and its brewery in Toll Gavel in 1797. The newly named Stephenson's Golden Ball Brewery was situated behind the Golden Ball pub and was rebuilt to the designs of Beverley architect William Hawe (1822-1897) when the main entrance was removed to Walkergate.

The 1851 Census recorded Thomas Clowes saddler and publican aged 29, his wife, a daughter, one female house servant and no less than ten lodgers at the Golden Ball, which gives some idea of its size and the nature of its trade.

The pub had a new shop-front fitted in 1911[114] and was sold to the Hull Brewery Co. Ltd along with the brewery in 1920. Even so, it was later made redundant in 1924 when the company received £1350 in compensation.

The brewery building survived until 1969 when it was demolished but the pub had been demolished after closure and Woolworth's shop now occupies the site.[115]

Golden Ball Yard, also known as Golden Ball Passage and colloquially as Woollie's Passage, has been in existence for at least 150 years, and runs between Walkergate and Toll Gavel where the brewery once stood.[116]

Writing of Beverley's signboards in 1939 *The Rambler* noted:

> *"The Golden Ball, an ancient house with centuries of history attached to it was closed through redundancy about twenty years ago. Its insignia was, as one would expect, in the form of a gilded ball, accompanied in miniature by the three tuns. These are oblong-shaped casks used for storing wines and other liqueurs."*[117]

---

[112] BOBE/6, 1925-5. East Riding of Yorkshire Council Archives.
[113] Ivan & Elizabeth Hall.
[114] BOBE/6, 1911-24. East Riding of Yorkshire Council Archives.

[115] Robert Barnard.
[116] David Sherwood.
[117] See bibliography.

The use of the symbolic three tuns was similar to the carved bunch of grapes often accompanying an inn sign to advertise that wines and spirits as well as ale, were available within.

SELECT VICTUALLERS
1924 Fred Hill
1921 Mrs Mary Watts
1905-16 Mrs Elizabeth Ramshaw
1877-99 Mrs Harriet Ramshaw
1872 Samuel Ramshaw
1858-70 William Ramshaw
1855 John McConnell Robson
1848-51 Thomas Clowes
1840-46 Benjamin Robson
1831-34 Thomas Clough
1828/29 Edward Osgerby Junior
1826 Edward Osgerby
1823 William Wadsworth
1814/15 William Watson
1784-91 Robert Thorp

Golden Fleece
Beckside.
See the Fleece.

Grapes Inn
Molescroft.
See the Molescroft Inn.

Green Dragon Inn
Market Place.
Also known as the Green Dragon & Black Swan

A reference in the Hull University Manuscripts and Archives Database (HUMAD)[118] recorded the Green Dragon in Lairgate in August 1745. This suggests that either there was already a pub in Lairgate named the Green Dragon or that the present Green Dragon may have originally *fronted* onto Lairgate. It is possible that the former malt house at the rear was the original *working end* of the pub or even the pub itself. It was suggested that *"the pub records"* dating from 1746 gave an older name for the Green Dragon; the *Malt House*.[119] There was a malt house at the rear of the property, which could account for the reasoning behind the assumption. There is evidence to suggest that the Green Dragon did face west and not east onto the Market Place.

A later HUMAD reference of September 1750 recorded the Green Dragon in Lare Gate [sic] being sold for £112 to John Tong innholder of Beverley.[120] An even more confusing notice appeared in the York Courant[121] of Tuesday December 25th 1770:

"TO BE LETT:
And entered upon at Midsummer next, situate in Beverley. All that commodious and well accustomed Inn, known by the sign of the Green Dragon & Black Swan, in the centre of the Market Place, with a Brewery, stabling, a coach house, and all suitable building thereto. Also a Back Door commanding different streets and roads, with an outlet into the west wood. For further particulars apply to Michael Staveley, Grocer in Beverley aforesaid, the owner". (sic)

This reference may suggest that the original Market Place side of the property was a grocer's and may later have become part of the pub itself. The reference to the *"Green Dragon & Black Swan"* may have been an interpretation of an heraldic inn-sign at the pub, possibly incorporating the coat of arms of the original land owner. This may have become abbreviated over the years to the *"Green Dragon"*.

[118] Ref. DDMM/2/127.
[119] Inn Places of Beverley (no source given).
[120] DDCV/15/127.
[121] Hull Local Studies Library.

The frontage hides a much older timber-framed core of the 17th Century.

The sign of the Green Dragon was described in a 1939 newspaper article:[122]

"The Green Dragon has a sign suspended from fancy beaten ironwork. The painted character has vanished and likewise the customary cluster of grapes at the end has followed suit. At one time, this was a station for one or two of the Stagecoach lines. In recent years a swing-board sign of much less artistic pretension has been hung to signify the Green Dragon."

Architectural historian David Neave writing for the revised Pevsner guide noted *"the mock timber facade of the Green Dragon, No.51 [Saturday Market] disguises the earlier origins of the building, which has some residual timber-framing"*.

This is confirmed by its Grade II listed building description in which it is suggested to be *"17th Century or earlier"*.[123]

The Census of 1851 recorded Elizabeth Harrison a widow aged 58, two daughters a female house servant and a lodger all present at the inn on the evening of the census.

The Beverley Guardian ran an advertisement in 1858 for:

*"GERMAN PIANO PLAYING
AT THE GREEN DRAGON,
(House cleared shortly before 12 o'clock. NB drinking in the Kitchen)"*.[124]

Plans by architect Frank Clayton of Beverley, drawn in 1908 showed the former *"stores and ash-place"* in Lairgate being altered into offices for the Green Dragon, which still exist in Lairgate.[125] It is clear that the Green Dragon holds many secrets and is undoubtedly an extremely old inn; it continues to enjoy good trade and is worth a visit if only to try and unravel its history for yourself.

SELECT VICTUALLERS
1987 Paul Thorp
1937-55 Mrs B A Jordan
1929 Harry James Porter
1915-21 Muscroft & Co.
1905 S B Heaps
1897-99 Mrs Mary Watson
1887-92 William Robert Watson
1882 John Sugdon
1872-79 Robert Skelton
1858-70 William Douthwaite
1846-55 Elizabeth Harrison
1840 James Watson
1806-34 John Walker
1791 Thomas Longbone
1750 John Tong

[122] Rambler, see bibliography.
[123] DoE serial No.9/339/69.
[124] Jan Crowther.

[125] BOBE/6, 1908-20 *"Alterations to the Green Dragon, Lairgate"* for Muscroft & Co. East Riding of Yorkshire Council Archives.

Grounds
Flemingate.
See Hodgson's.

Grovehill Hotel
Holme Church Lane.
Also known as the Grovehill Tavern.

The Grovehill pub, No.183 Holme Church Lane was built for Moor's & Robsons' brewery in 1907[126] and took its licence from the redundant Nag's Head near the old Grovehill Ferry crossing (the Nag's Head had also been listed, very confusingly, as the Grovehill Tavern in 1855 and one of the two names may have been a colloquial version that survived as the official name). G Pape & Sons built it at a cost of £1895.[127]

The large building, which still dominates its surroundings in Grovehill Road, is a good example of the confident if not over stylish, architecture of the Edwardian era. A large Bowling Green that stood at the rear of the building has now sadly gone but some fine details do remain from the original build. A dramatic stone entrance and some original frosted lettered glass windows to the bar and smoke room are amongst the most impressive.

SELECT VICTUALLERS
1987 Glen Blackwell
1955-67 A E Roberts
1929-37 John William Whitehead
1915-16 William Whitehead

The bold architecture of the Grovehill Tavern's main entrance.

The Grovehill Hotel was built in 1907 at a cost of £1,895. Its bold architecture is typical of that period, and some original details remain such as the frosted glass windows of the "public bar" and the "smoke room".

Hall Garth Inn
Minster Yard South.
See the Admiral Duncan.

Hart
Wednesday Market.
See the Queen's Head.

---

[126] BOBE/6, 1907-8. East Riding of Yorkshire Council Archives.
[127] Robert Barnard.

Hayride

'Butterfly Meadows'

A typically modern pub in the *new* Molescroft area, which opened in 1997.

Hodgson's

Flemingate.
Also known as the Grounds.

Fleming House was an early 19th Century villa which latterly became the recreation club of nearby tanners Hodgson's Ltd. Planning approval for the conversion of the derelict house into the "Grounds" was given in December 1996 but work was not underway until August 1997. Although most welcomed the plans, particularly the immediate locals who had for many years to suffer the dangers of living next to a derelict building, an 87-name petition and long delays by the local councillors in granting approval for internal alterations and planning consent dragged the process on and on.
Although a Grade II listed building it had been noted as one of Beverley's worst eyesores (its condition had been the subject of local newspaper debates since the early 1990s) when entrepreneur Danny Banks of Weba Leisure Ltd. stepped in with plans which he promised would preserve its Georgian appearance.
It eventually opened in September 1997 and had allegedly cost approximately £500,000. Currently still enjoying measured success the Grounds was fittingly re-named Hodgson's in spring 2000 and is a very pleasant addition to the still neglected Flemingate area.

Holderness Hotel

Toll Gavel.
Also known as the Sign of the Horns, the Blue Boar & Horns and the Blue Boar.

The York Courant newspaper of 20th September 1768 ran a notice for an auction *"to be held at the house of Mr Davidson, the sign of the Horns in Beverley"*. In March 1770 another notice mentioned *"the Blue Boar in Beverley"* and in June 1770 *"the house of Mr Thomas Davidson, the sign of the Blue Boar & Horns in Beverley"*.
Landress Lane, just south of the pub used to be known as *Horns* Lane and was almost certainly an early reference to the Blue Boar & Horns[128] whose property boundary ran almost its entire length.
The sign of the Blue Boar was often linked with coats of arms and has also had links with the Wars of the Roses whereas the Beverley references were all probably linked with hunting; *hunting* horns, the *hunted* Boar and the Holderness *Hunt*. The Blue Boar was also recorded as an excise office in 1823 and was renamed the Holderness Inn in 1829.[129] A slightly later advertisement dated 26th March 1830 in the Hull Advertiser recorded a:

> *"**CAPITAL INN**, at **BEVERLEY**, to be let.*
> *For a term of 7 – 10 years, may be entered upon immediately. That old-established and well accustomed inn, formerly know by the name of the Blue Boar, but now called the Holderness Hotel, situate in the most public part of Beverley; all the York, Hull and Scarborough coaches passing it daily, and very near the Market-Place, comprimising every accommodation, and having a spacious yard, with stabling for 60 horses.*

---

[128] VCH.
[129] Hull Advertiser 22.5.1829.

Upwards of £500 have lately been expended on the house, which is in excellent repair, and full of business, and well known as one of the best-accustomed houses at Fairs and Markets.
Rent and Particulars: Mr. Edward Wilson (premises)".
(sic)

In Beverley's keenly fought 19th Century elections it was frequented by Liberals.

In the Census of 1851 Hannah Wilson was resident at the inn aged 67 with two sons, one a druggist and one a grocer, four unmarried daughters and an ostler for the horses.

In the 20th Century the horses were supplemented with motor cars and the Holderness Garage was situated at the rear of the pub. An advertisement from circa 1910 listed many other attractions of the pub including large dining rooms for *"luncheons and teas"*, stabling, billiards, petrol supply and servicing as well as being the headquarters of the East Riding Golf Club and the headquarters of the Imperial Yeomanry.

The hotel ceased to be listed in the trade directories after 1930 having been purchased by H Scofield & Co. who added a new *"shop front"* in the ground floor in March 1931.[130] Most of the unchanged upper storeys of the imposing building are still clearly visible today. The building was awarded Grade II listed building status in 1969.[131]

This photograph produced circa 1905 for advertising purposes shows the elegant frontage of the Holderness Hotel, which had been known as the Blue Boar and earlier the Blue Boar & Horns. (Beverley Local Studies Library)

HOLDERNESS HOTEL
TOLL-GAVEL,
BEVERLEY.

JOHN CHARTER,

Begs most respectfully to inform his Friends and the Public that he has taken the above old-established HOTEL, and solicits their patronage and support.

WINES & SPIRITS OF THE BEST QUALITY.

EXCELLENT STABLING AND COACH HOUSES.

COMMERCIAL GENTLEMEN and FAMILIES will find every convenience and accommodation at the above HOTEL.

An OMNIBUS attends the arrival of every Train.

An advertisement of circa 1858 for the Holderness Hotel. Note "an omnibus attends the arrival of every train".

[130] BOBE/6, 1931-9. East Riding of Yorkshire Council Archives.
[131] DoE serial No.9/361/69.

A later photograph of the Holderness Hotel circa 1925 after the Hull Brewery had taken charge of the premises.

SELECT VICTUALLERS
1929-30 Miss Teresa Curling
1925 Christian Henry Wm Smythe
1921 James William Arthur Renton
1915-16 Christopher May
1905 Charles Jarvis Naylor
1899 Holderness Hotel
1882-97 Elizabeth Anne Watson
1864-79 Thomas Watson
1861 William Dee
1858-59 John Charter
1855 William Clark
1846-51 Hannah Wilson
1831-40 Thomas Wilson
1828/29 Edward Wilson
1814-26 William Richardson
1768-70 Thomas Davidson

Holderness Tavern

Norwood.
See the Valiant Soldier.

The Hull Advertiser of August 10th 1839 noted: *"For sale, Holderness Tavern, formerly the Valiant Soldier"*.

Horns (*Sign of the*)

Toll Gavel.
See the Holderness Hotel.

Humber Keel

Coltman Avenue.

A typically utilitarian post Second World War pub (built circa 1954)[132] that has been altered but nevertheless continues

The Humber Keel, shown here in 1987, can be seen as a good example of period public house architecture. Its clean lines although now somewhat altered are still a fair indicator of early 1950s pub design. (Frank Pinfold)

to serve its locals well. It can be seen as a fair example of 1950s pub architecture and boasts a very large bar.

King's Arms

North Bar Within.

Two 17th Century coins or tokens known as pub checks exist for the King's Arms dated 1664 and 1666, which bear the legend; *"George Lamplugh at the King's Arms"*. They relate to a property that was located at the north side of St. Mary's Church (see Thomas Malton junior's illustration of 1780 in Old Beverley page 23) that was demolished circa 1810-20.
In 1784 Francis Weldon, innholder, was recorded in a corporation lease at *"an inn called the King's Arms on the east side of Within North Barr"*.[133]

---

[132] Inn Places of Beverley.
[133] DDBC/16/221, East Riding of Yorkshire Council Archives.

The inn was relocated to No.28 North Bar Within, a property that still survives on the east side of North Bar Within (currently two shops, one a sports shop), complete with bracket from which the inn sign once hung.

The 1851 Census recorded Sarah Akrill aged 70, her daughter, an ostler and *boots*, a chambermaid and a barmaid at the King's Arms.

The following is an advertisement from the Beverley Guardian, dated 9th January 1858:

> ### "KING'S ARMS COMMERCIAL AND FAMILY HOTEL,
> #### NORTH BAR STREET, BEVERLEY.
> *GEORGE SMELT begs to tender his best thanks to his friends for the kind support he has received since occupying the above Hotel, and respectfully announces that he has retired from, and disposed of the same along with the Cab and Posting business, to Mr. J. C. PICKERING, V.S., whom he can confidently recommend to their notice, and for whom he solicits a continuance of the patronage bestowed upon himself for a long series of years.*
> *J.C. PICKERING, V.S., on entering the above Concern, respectfully announces to the Public that the utmost attention, as heretofore, will be paid to the comfort of all those who may honour him with their patronage, and every endeavour will be made, by supplying articles of first-rate quality only, to secure a continuance of the patronage so liberally bestowed on his predecessor.*
> *Cabs, Gigs, and Horses, for hire, on the shortest notice, and at reasonable Fares.*
> *N.B.- VETERINARY INFIRMARY AS USUAL."* (sic)

During the horse-fairs that were regularly held in Beverley, the King's Arms was noted for its trading and was host to many foreign dealers as were many other hotels in the town.

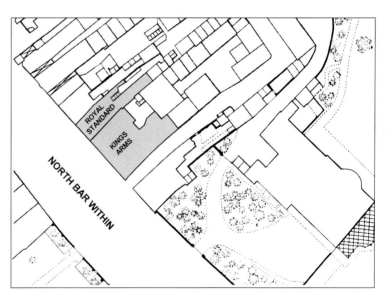

A circa 1858 advertisement for the Kings Arms.

A map of circa 1890 showing the Kings Arms. Note the house, now demolished, at the south side of Coombs' Yard.

This picture postcard view shows North Bar Within during the winter of 1904. To the right are the Kings Arms and the Royal Standard, both Grade II listed buildings. All of the buildings shown have survived.

The Beverley Guardian reported in November 1859:

"A fine drove of Scotch Ponies at the King's Arms Inn brought direct from Brough Hill by Anakin brothers of Thirsk were all sold at prices varying from £12 to £25". (sic)

During the 1870s and into the 1880s the King's Arms also served as a posting house.

The King's Arms was made redundant in 1926 when £1000 was paid in compensation to the owners.

The signboard of the King's Arms was described in 1939 as *"a humble sign of the Heraldic Order, but the badge of the reigning Sovereign, which it commemorated in the olden days, has disappeared"*.[134] A postcard view of the King's Arms of circa 1905 showed that the board had been gone for some years as it showed only the hanging bracket.

The property was awarded Grade II listed building status in 1969.[135]

SELECT VICTUALLERS
1925 Henry Gadd
1915-21 John Cupit
1899-1905 George Allison
1897 John Payne
1889-92 Miss Fanny Sharp
1872-82 Thomas Barnes
1864-69 William Boyes
1858-59 George Smelt
1846-51 Sarah Ackrill
1814-40 William Ackrill
1806 William Kirkhouse
1791 Ann Kirman
1784 Francis Weldon
1664-66 George Lamplugh

---

[134] Rambler, see bibliography.
[135] DoE serial No.9/233/69.

King's Head Hotel

Market Place.

The King's Head is a Grade II listed building[136] and is a good example of Beverley's many historic inns. Its listed building description suggests the fabric of the building to be of the mid-18th Century but was written in 1950; more recent analysis[137] has revealed that it could easily be of the late 17th Century. It had probably been an inn for many years before its first appearance in the trade directories from circa 1806, and was up for sale by 1811:[138]

> *"KING'S HEAD INN*
> *To be Sold by Private Contract,*
> *All that well accustomed and eligibly situated Public House or Inn, on the East side of the Market Place in Beverley, known by the sign of the King's Head Inn. Lately occupied by Israel Marshall, deceased.*
> *The stables are capable of containing accommodation for 60 horses at least. The premises have the advantage of a road or thoroughfare from the Market Place to a street called Walkergate.*
> *The purchaser will be required to take at a fair appraisement and valuation, the brewing utensils and all the beds and furniture now occupied with the said inn."* (sic)

It was sold again in 1827 and October 1841:[139]

> *"To let the King's Head with brewhouse, large dining room and upwards of 20 beds, ground plot 1,200 square yards. R. Clark – the owner"*

The census of 1851 recorded David Morley aged 53, his wife, one son David (a bank clerk), three daughters, a male servant and a female house servant at the King's Head. During Mr Morley's tenancy the King's Head was one of Beverley's many posting houses.

The Pevsner guide states simply:

> *"The King's Head Hotel … mid 18th Century, altered in the early 19th Century. Its distinctive three-storey five bay stuccoed facade has a Doric porch and above a balcony to round-arched window flanked by coupled pilasters".*

The pub was later extended to encompass adjoining offices and the new bar has been known by a variety of names including the Sovereign Lounge and the Market Tap. It does retain some original details but inevitably much has been lost during refurbishment.

The Kings Head Hotel in the spring of 2001. Note the addition of bay windows and an "olde inn-sign". Although some original details have been preserved the interior of the pub is now completely changed.

---

[136] DoE serial No.9/333/50.
[137] Royal Commission on Historic Monuments 1982.
[138] York Courant, 16.12.1811.
[139] Eastern Counties Herald (via Robert Barnard)

The Kings Head Hotel in Saturday Market in a 1920s photograph by Hull photographer Harry Abba. Note the doorway of the building to its right, which sadly has been moved to the corner of the property to make way for a modern shop front (see page 53).

SELECT VICTUALLERS
1987 Paul Brooks
1965-75 A C Barnes
1955 F Mansford
1943 H A E Stephenson
1937-39 Percy Stephenson
1929 Mrs Eliza Bell
1915-21 George U Hodgson
1905 Edith Ellen Farnill
1899 Kings Head Hotel
1892-97 Alfred Hoyle
1889 Francis Otter
1882 George Carr
1877-79 John Walker
1872 George Bielby
1870 T Dunning
1869 C Taylor
1867 George Oates
1840-64 David Morley
1828-34 Robert Clark
1814-27 Robert Witty
1810 Israel Marshall
1806 William Witty

Lady Le Gros
Norwood.

Although it had been listed in the trade directories as an un-named beerhouse since at least 1874[140] the Lady Le Gros was first noted *by name* around 1881. The census of that year recorded Samuel Peacock beerhouse keeper aged 36, his wife Sarah aged 27 and their four children, with Jane Marshall aged 15 a general servant all present at the pub. It is likely that Samuel Peacock was the first victualler and opened the pub around 1870 when he arrived in the area from his native town of Burstwick (his first child was born in Beverley in 1873/4 according to the 1881 census).

The precise reason for the naming of the pub has been lost in the mists of time, however Samuel Peacock had been a cow-keeper as well as a beerhouse keeper (1892 directory); could the "Lady Le Gros" have been his *retort* to the nearby Durham Ox?

The current premises of the Lady Le Gros are the result of various alterations, additions and rebuilding of a simple farmhouse, although none of the *original* building remains.

Plans drawn in March 1893 for *"additions and alterations to the Lady Le Gros Beerhouse in Norwood"*[141] show the original building was a simple three-bay farmhouse facing west with its gable end to the road. The alterations of 1893 added buildings to its north side including a new kitchen, bedroom, cellar, wash-house, pantry, cart shed and two privvies.

The Lady Le Gros as she appeared in 1987. (Frank Pinfold)

---

[140] John Ward's Almanac, Beverley Local Studies Library.
[141] For Charles Darley of Thorne, ref.293 East Riding of Yorkshire Council Archives.

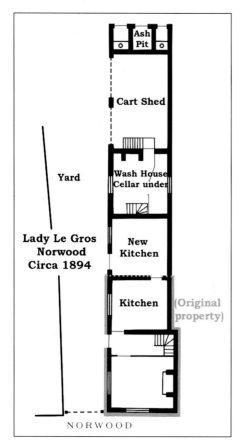

Lady Le Gros
Norwood
Circa 1894

NORWOOD

Ash Pit

Cart Shed

Yard

Wash House
Cellar under

New
Kitchen

Kitchen (Original property)

A plan of the Lady Le Gros beerhouse as it appeared circa 1894. Note the original farmhouse building (marked in grey) was adjacent to the footpath and was demolished in the 1930s to create a car park when the buildings were being rebuilt set-back from the road line.

In 1936 more alterations involved an almost total rebuilding of the pub, and the whole of the original farmhouse was demolished to set the building back from the road in its current position.

SELECT VICTUALLERS
1987 Malcolm Firth
1975 G Sanderson
1967 J T Cook
1965 L A Cattermole

[142] HUMAD ref. DDCV/15/174

1943-55 J S Shawler
1929-39 Charles Henry King
1874-1928 Samuel Peacock

Lincoln Arms
Lincoln Way
Also known as the Sanctuary.

This modern pub on the Keldgate Park Estate, opened in 1988 as the Sanctuary, may have taken its name from the ancient Sanctuary Stones, which stood around Beverley. Three of these survive, one not far from the pub, in Bentley. It was renamed the Lincoln Arms in 2000.

Lion & Lamb
Ladygate.

Writing in the updated *Pevsner* David Neave says:

" *a typical success was the retention and restoration of No.11 Ladygate, externally an unpretentious building, but late medieval with timber-framing exposed on the first floor and to the side elevation along Sylvester Lane. Again a long narrow medieval plot.*"

It is clear that the former Lion & Lamb building was medieval and had probably been an inn from a very early date. A draft conveyance and assignment of the property dated 21st November 1786 records that *"Robert Dalton innkeeper and wife Elizabeth, Alice Stephenson spinster and John Lockwood gent"* passed the property to *"John Tuting cordwainer and Isabel Doughty spinster, all of Beverley…(Lion and Lamb Inn on the east side of Ladygate)"*.[142]

This map of the north end of Ladygate shows the location of the Lion & Lamb beerhouse and its neighbours in an area of Beverley that was well served with public houses. This was probably due to its close proximity to the market areas.

In 1858 the Beverley Guardian ran a concerned article with a description of Sylvester Lane at night:

"When the pubs close on a Saturday night people congregate there and use bad and disgusting language. The watchman on duty is ignored when he tells them to go home."[143]

The census of 1881 listed William Stephenson as licensed victualler at the small pub with his wife and son, and one female general servant.

The Lion & Lamb, which held a full licence closed when it was made redundant in 1909 and compensation of £656 was paid to the owners John Smith's Brewery of Tadcaster.

Thankfully the remaining property was awarded Grade II listed building status in 1980[144] and is afforded some protection from any future threat.

SELECT VICTUALLERS
1897-1909 Walter Whitehead
1889-92 Robert Sanderson
1887 John William Richardson
1881-82 William Stephenson
1858-79 Frederick Voase
1840-55 John Taylor
1823-34 Joseph Turley
1814/15 Joseph Turner
1784 Richard Tuting
Pre 1786 Robert Dalton

Litchfield Arms

Toll Gavel.
Also known as the Red Lion.

The Census of 1851 recorded innkeeper Henry Anthony aged 44, his wife, five daughters, his mother in law, one female house servant, a traveller and *militia staff* present at the Red Lion on the night of the census.

The Red Lion had an inn-sign *"with an image of the said heraldic beast, which was later replaced by a model of the beast"* according to *"Rambler- an old time scribe"*, writing in 1939.[145]

The Red Lion had undergone alterations late in 1888[146] following the death of owner Mr Johnson and it is likely the premises were sold by his daughter following his demise. This pub was another that was purchased by Robert Attwood Litchfield in the 1890s and could be said to have been his flagship premises and was consequently renamed as the Litchfield Arms.

In 1899 he submitted plans drawn by a Hull Builder & Contractor, for *"a public house and shop at No.30 Toll Gavel"*.[147] This involved a complete remodelling and re-fronting of the premises in typical high Victorian style.

In 1912/13 Miss Lucy Litchfield, presumably a daughter had a tobacconist's at No.32 Toll Gavel, next door to the Litchfield, which was No.30.

The Litchfield, which closed in 1972, is partly preserved on the first floor level above the present modern building society and remnants of the impressive frontage are visible on the ground floor. Plans from the rebuild of 1899 show that the pub had a wholesale department and a surviving example of a bottle marked with Litchfield's name and monogram (author's collection) suggests that beer and spirits were available for off-sales by the public.

SELECT VICTUALLERS
1972 M Battersby
1967-71 F E Battersby
1965 R Bates
1955 A E Johnson
1937-39 Alexander A Slesser
1929 Thomas William Cressey
1921-29 George Henry West

---

[143] Reference from Jan Crowther
[144] DoE serial No.9/127/80.
[145] See bibliography.

[146] BOBE/6, 1888-211. East Riding of Yorkshire Council Archives.
[147] BOBE/6, 1899-2. J Hancock, Builder & Contractor, Steam Saw Mills, 38 Waterloo Street Hull. East Riding of Yorkshire Council Archives.

1899-1915 Robert Attwood Litchfield
1892 J May
1893 Miss Ann Johnson
1889 William Cotcheifer
1887 Richard Hutham
1882 Samuel Bielby
1881 William Stitt
1879 Hugh Jack
1877 Thomas Tomlinson
1869-72 William Mason
1867 Thomas Coverdale
1861-64 Edward Stephenson
1858-59 John Sanderson
1848-55 Henry Anthony
1846 John Westerby
1840 John Hutton
1834 William Atkinson
1823-32 John Atkinson
1814/15 Mary Shores
1791 Aaron Shores

It would take very little imagination to picture the frontage of the Litchfield Arms beneath the impressive triple gables of the surviving upper storeys in Toll Gavel. The left third of the building was the tobacconist's shop also owned by Robert Atwood Litchfield.

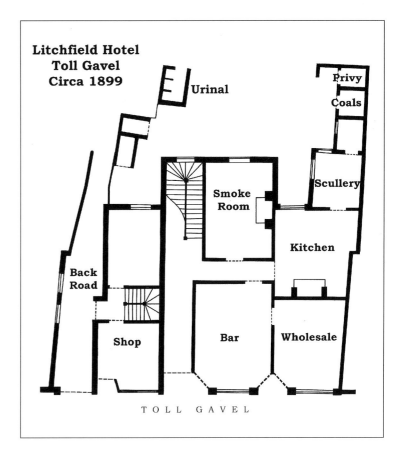

A floor plan of the Litchfield of circa 1899, which shows clearly how the original building (centre) had expanded north into adjoining property (probably in 1888 when it was still known as the Red Lion).

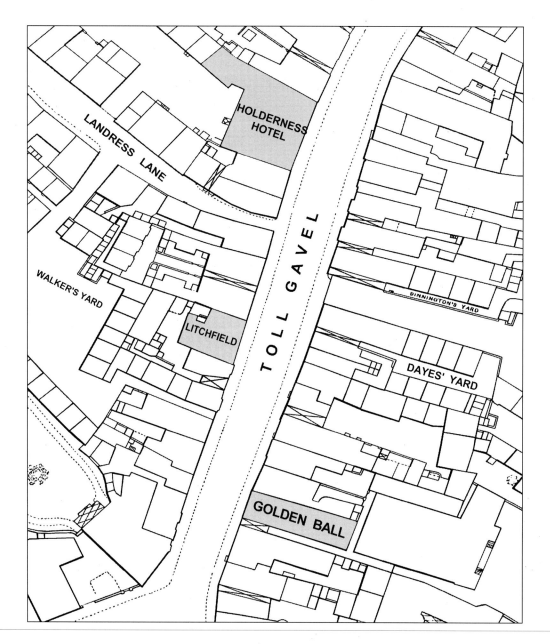

A map showing part of Toll Gavel circa 1898 showing an interesting and colourful cluster of pubs; the Golden Ball, the Lichfield (formerly the Red Lion) and the Holderness Hotel (formerly the Blue Boar). Note the many small yards containing tiny dwelling houses.

Lord Nelson Inn

Flemingate.
Also known as the Admiral Lord Nelson.

The name "Lord Nelson" must surely rank amongst the top ten pub names in England.

The average tourist or *Beverlonian* probably passes Beverley's unassuming Lord Nelson unaware that it is probably one of Beverley's oldest pub buildings.

The building has undergone some alteration; in 1912 a new *"smoke room and scullery"* were created and a serving counter fitted in the *"tap room"* (by architects Bromet & Thorman of Tadcaster).[148]

Even in its altered state it was still considered of sufficient historical and architectural importance to be awarded the prestigious Grade II star listing by the Secretary of State in 1980[149] in whose description it is described as *"probably late 17th Century"*.

David Neave writing in the updated *Pevsner* states:

"the stuccoed 19th Century façade of the Lord Nelson Inn disguises a much earlier building which is revealed in the first floor studding and braces exposed on the east elevation, and in the good late 15th Century crown post roof "(of No.15 incorporated in the same range of buildings).[150]

Other historians have suggested that it was established as an inn circa 1620[151] but this has to be confirmed. It appeared in the trade directories circa 1814, only a matter of years after the death of Lord Nelson. It is very likely that the Lord Nelson had another name prior to this.

Mair & Clarke, brewers of Wilbert Lane owned the Lord Nelson by 1813.[152] Part of the marriage settlement (dated 9th May 1816) of Dorothy Mair (widow of John Mair, brewer) and William Edwards of Beverley, a saddler, was Dorothy Mair's *"moiety of brewery (Mair and Clarke), her personal estate; Lord Nelson Inn & a brewery in Appletree Lane"*.[153]

The Census of 1851 recorded Robert Spink, a millwright and victualler aged 35, his wife, baby daughter and one female general servant present at the inn.

The Beverley Guardian ran an article in 1858 re- an inquest on a 42 year old Keel owner who *"Partook of a glass of beer, sang a song and fell down dead"* in the Lord Nelson Inn.

Writing of Beverley's signboards the *Rambler* noted in 1939:

"The Lord Nelson, in Flemingate had an excellent hanging painting of that great Admiral of England. This got severely weather beaten but continued to fulfil its mission of depicting Britain's great Naval Hero, until its removal some years ago".[154]

The unassuming Lord Nelson Inn, shown here in 2001. Its stuccoed façade hides an older core of at least the 17th Century. A Grade II star listed building.

[148] BOBE/6, 1912-8 for John Smith & Co. East Riding of Yorkshire Council Archives.
[149] DoE serial No.10/52/80.
[150] Page 318.

[151] Inn Places of Beverley (no source given).
[152] Robert Barnard.
[153] HUMAD ref. DDCV/15/375.
[154] See bibliography.

It would be interesting to remove the stuccoed plaster from the front of the Lord Nelson and gain any more clues to its original appearance.

The west elevation of the group of buildings incorporating the Lord Nelson Inn (Nos.13-15 Flemingate) revealing the true age of the buildings in the exposed studding and braces. The oldest of the buildings shown are of the 15th Century.

SELECT VICTUALLERS
1987 David Henderson
1967 G Cook
1965 J Ralphs
1915-39 Edward James Turner
1905 J Turner
1892-99 Thomas Bielby
1889 Robert Stuart
1887 Samuel Bielby
1882 Dan Secker

1879 Mrs Sarah Firth
1877 Henry Firth
1872 Robert Booth
1867-70 William Pape
1864 John Priestman
1858-59 William Wilson
1848-55 Robert Spink
1834-46 William Salmon
1823-32 Mathew John Moor
1814-15 John Moor

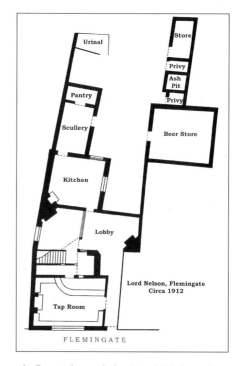

A floor plan of the Lord Nelson Inn as it appeared c1912. The plan shows that the "beer store" of the pub was situated in the very oldest part of the buildings, known to be 15th Century.

The Malt Shovel in Walkergate (demolished 1967) shown here in a photograph of the 1950s. The pub at one time had a hanging sign depicting a maltster's shovel according to a newspaper article of 1939. (Beverley Local Studies Library)

"Malt House"
Lairgate.
See the Green Dragon.

Malt Shovel
Walkergate.

Writing in 1939, *the Rambler* said of the Malt Shovel:

> *"The Malt Shovel was at one time prominently emblemised by a Maltster's Shovel, in the front of the licensed house in Walkergate bearing that name."*[155]

John Smith & Co. owned the building latterly and plans show they had altered the interior in 1902.[156] The plans and a photograph of circa 1950 show the pub to have been a simple three-bay building similar in appearance to the Buck Inn. To the left of the central entrance and hall was a *"Tap Room"* and to the right a *"Smoke Room"*.

The pub closed in the early 1940s and the building was demolished many years later for the *New Walkergate* development of June 1967.[157]

SELECT VICTUALLERS
1937-39 Herbert Pearce Duffill
1915-29 Andrew Windle
1905 Mrs H Smith
1897-99 John Robinson
1893 Mrs Jane Harrison
1892 H Barns
1879-89 John Lee
1877 W Beautiman
1872 Thomas Cobb
1869-70 Thos Wilson
1867 Benjamin Ross

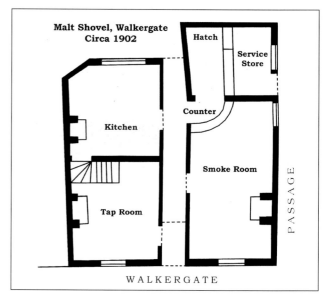

A floor plan of the Malt Shovel circa 1902 showing a simple layout common to many small pubs of the time. Note the "off licence" at the rear of the smoke room entered from the side passage.

Mariners Arms
Flemingate.
Also known as the Plough.

The Census of 1851 recorded Martin Lascelles innkeeper and blacksmith aged 42, his wife and two sons present at the Mariners Arms.

The authors of The Inn Places of Beverley stated that the Mariners building is a rebuild of an earlier pub the Plough, however the evidence *on the ground* i.e. the building itself, has features and brickwork (visible at the rear) that could easily be of the late 18th Century. It seems very likely that the present Mariners Arms is the same building as the Plough.

---

[155] See bibliography.
[156] BOBE/6, 1902-13 East Riding of Yorkshire Council Archives.
[157] Beverley Guardian 23.6.67.

The study produced by the Royal Commission on Historic Monuments concluded the building is of 1780-1860 and it is safe to say the present building retains much of the original pub.

The Mariners has Grade II listed building status,[158] and in its official description of 1987 it was suggested that it is *"of the early 19th Century"*. The pub changed name circa 1870 to become the Mariners Arms.

Gapp's Yard was located on Beckside, near the Mariners Arms and was extant during the 1890s.[159] It was almost certainly named after George Gapp, victualler of the pub during the 1880s and 1890s or another member of his family. He was later (circa 1899) listed as a lodging-house keeper at the corner of Holme Church Lane. His predecessors at the Mariners Arms were the Loft family (firstly from 1784-1846 as the Plough and later from 1870-80); Loft's Yard was mentioned in the 1881 Census. It is possible that the two yards were one and the same but renamed by subsequent landlords.

Alterations were carried out to the Mariners Arms by the owners Darley's Thorne Brewery in the spring of 1919 when a new and enlarged kitchen area was added (architect Richard Whiteing of Ladygate Beverley).[160] Later alterations meant the loss of the original three rooms and now the Mariners has the ubiquitous large bar.

The original small front rooms of the pub were more evidence of the origins of the pub. The 1852 Ordnance Survey plans show the Plough as a small beerhouse; two bays wide literally one house. By the 1890 plan, noted as the Mariners Arms, it had been extended to take in the properties to its east and west. This expansion gave the Mariners its current six-bay appearance, and on examination it is clearly three small houses made into one property.

SELECT VICTUALLERS
1987 Ian Atkinson
1965-75 H Craggs
1939 John William Clapham
1915-37 Edward Harrison Butt
1897-1905 George William Hodgson
1882-93 George Gapp
1877-79 Edwin Loft
1870-72 William Loft
1864-67 William Morrell
1858-59 Robert Richardson
1855 Solomon Sollit
1848-51 Martin Lascelles
1784-1846 Samuel Loft

Market Cross Tavern
Market Place.

A coffee tavern, which opened in the Saturday Market in 1878. *"Tea, coffee, cocoa, loaf & cheese, hot peas – all at 2d each."*[161]

In a bid to encourage temperance the church supported coffee taverns and this was the first of Beverley's two known taverns (See also the British Workman). By 1889 they were part of the Beverley Coffee Tavern Ltd.

In the first part of the 20th Century Mrs W.H. Rutherford took charge of the coffee tavern and it was to become known locally as Rutherford's Cafe. A photograph of 1904 shows the building looking remarkably like a pub.

A coin known as a *refreshment token* exists for the Market Cross Tavern.

Market Hotel
Norwood
See the Drovers Arms.

---

[158] DoE serial No.11/67/87.
[159] David Sherwood.
[160] BOBE/6, 1919-6. East Riding of Yorkshire Council Archives.

[161] A Beverley Chronology page 11.

A 1904 view of the former Market Cross Coffee Tavern in Saturday Market Place. To entice drinkers away from the inns and taverns the coffee-taverns often disguised themselves as pubs and the Market Cross made a good effort.

Market Tap
Saturday Market
See the Kings Head

Marquis of Wellington
Molescroft.
See the Molescroft Inn.

Molescroft Inn
Molescroft Road.
Also known as the Marquis of Wellington, the Battle of Trafalgar and the Grapes.

A licensed house later called the Marquis of Wellington (simply the Wellington in 1823) was recorded in Molescroft from at least 1754.[162] As an alehouse it served the hamlet of Molescroft, which had only 124 inhabitants in 1840.[163] It appears to have been re-named the Battle of Trafalgar (simply the *Trafalgar* in some directories) in the early 19th Century in recognition of Nelson's victory over Napoleon in 1805. Known colloquially as the Molescroft Inn it began to be *officially* listed as such in the trade directories of the 1870s.

It was also listed as the Grapes for a time in some trade directories; this was a name given to many pubs with the sign of the grapes hanging from their signboard. In actual fact it probably retained its original name throughout.

The census of 1881 recorded the new victualler of the pub just arrived from Lincolnshire; George Willows innkeeper aged 40, his wife, three sons and a general servant at the inn. During alterations in the early 1980s a small inglenook fireplace was discovered behind a cupboard, sadly the alterations meant the loss of some smaller rooms to create one large "L" shaped room.[164] The pub is now greatly enlarged and has encompassed former dwellings to its north. The Molescroft is now a popular *eating place* as well as continuing its duties as a *local*, which it has performed for around 250 years.

---

[162] VCH page 284.
[163] William White's History & Gazetteer of the East Riding of Yorkshire.
[164] Inn Places of Beverley.

The Molescroft Inn (formerly the Battle of Trafalgar, the Marquis of Wellington and the Grapes) shown here in a photograph of circa 1925. The Molescroft has served the population of the former village of Molescroft for over two hundred and fifty years.

SELECT VICTUALLERS
1987 Peter Hampton
1943-67 E Gallagher
1937-39 William L Gibson
1929 Mrs Elizabeth Taylor
1915-21 Peter Hunsley
1887-1905 James Hewitt
1881-82 George Willows
1879 Frank Parker
1872 Mrs Sarah Hardbattle
1858-64 John Ketten Hardbattle
1855 William Hardbattle
1823-40 Francis Johnson

The extended Molescroft Inn shown here in 1987. (Frank Pinfold)

Monks Walk

Highgate.
Also known as the George, the George & Dragon and the Old George & Dragon.

The *"George in Highgate"* was mentioned in 1686 according to the Victoria County History for Beverley, however an earlier reference is to be found in a document dated 7th July 1658 recorded a:

"Quitclaim: Richard Johnson of Bishop Burton gent' to Hugh Bethell jnr' of Ryse esq. ...Messuage called the George in High Street alias the Londoner Street and a close (Lobley Lane to the North) in Beverley."[165]

John Mair, an innholder and probably the John Mair listed as a brewer in Wilbert Lane, married Elizabeth Story in 1802. He was also known to have been brewing at the George & Dragon Highgate. Other members of the Mair family were also brewers but it is not clear if the George & Dragon, Highgate contained a brewery or was their residential address.[166]

The Census of 1851 recorded Thomas Robinson aged 42, his wife, one son, one daughter, a female house servant and a labourer present at the George & Dragon.

There were additions to the George & Dragon in January 1895 for the owners Chas. Darley & Co.[167]

George and Dragon Yard is still in existence today to the rear of the pub although its main entrance is in Eastgate. The entrance from Highgate may have been known as Blizzard's Passage as it was recorded in the late 19th Century at the time when the victualler of the George & Dragon was Robert Blizzard, who was there from 1887 until at least 1916.

Although at first glance the property appears to be of the early 19th Century it has been re-fronted during the 18th Century and medieval buildings are evident on both sides of the passage as well as details dated 1671.[168]

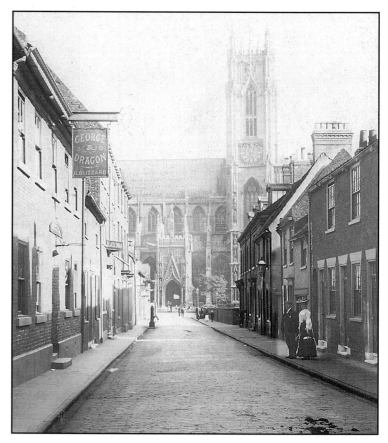

Highgate looking south towards the Minster circa 1905. To the right are the former George & Dragon (now the Monks Walk) and beyond the Black Swan, which closed in 1909. Note the old water pump at the end of the street. (Beverley Local Studies Library)

[165] HUMAD ref. DDGE/3/58
[166] Robert Barnard
[167] BOBE/6, 1895-1. East Riding of Yorkshire Council Archives.

[168] Beverley Friary Trust notes 1977.

In 1995 major investigations took place on the site and the following are extracts from a report featured in the Hull Daily Mail of 13th May 1995:

"A hidden treasure-trove of history has been discovered during work on a pub. Layers of plaster have been stripped away at the Monks Walk in Beverley to reveal a series of medieval cottages within the building. Roof and wall timbers dating back as early as 1420 have been uncovered and evidence of the medieval craftsmen's handiwork can clearly be seen. Among the finds are roof timbers hewn roughly out of whole tree trunks, in what is thought to be the only roof of its kind in the town. Conservation experts and pub bosses were stunned by the finds, which came to light through plans to alter and extend the building.

The pub in the shadow of Beverley Minster is an important Listed Building and planning chiefs insisted on an investigation of the site, parts of which have not been used for years, before they granted consent.

A team of experts from the Royal Commission on Historical Monuments was called in and has been monitoring the finds. Now the pub's owners are working with conservationists to preserve the historic features as part of their plans to convert the building into a luxury hotel.

They believe the building will become a major tourist attraction, and hope to create a museum as part of their scheme. Mr Roland Craft, Managing Director of Viking International, which owns the pub, said the wealth of history unearthed on the site had amazed even the top national experts; "Everybody was overwhelmed. The Royal Commission do not come up to Beverley very often, but they put a team in to investigate the whole site," said Mr Craft. "We have had people in to look at it who just don't believe what is here."

Among the experts who have examined the finds is Mr Rod Mackey, local representative for the Council for British Archaeology. He said the finds were an exciting discovery; "I have tried to analyse what I could see, and as far as I can make out the building is an 18th Century frontage which has been clad onto what appear to be two timber-framed buildings that span the passage, which was a medieval street. I think people realised that there would be timber framed buildings behind the 18th Century frontage but what is surprising is the extent to which it has survived. It has rotted off at ground level but above that everything else is still there."

The Monks Walk (formerly the George & Dragon) in 1987. During alterations in 1995 a series of medieval structures were revealed within the building dating from the 15th Century. Worth a visit to view the impressive medieval roof timbers in the dining area and many other features. (Frank Pinfold)

Needless to say the Monks Walk has been a Grade II *star* listed building since the 1950s.[169]

A fire closed the Monks Walk from late 2000 until its welcome reopening in April 2001. Thankfully no serious damage was done.

SELECT VICTUALLERS
1987 Gary Walton
1937-39 Harold Staveley
1929 Thomas Jobson
1921 Mrs Mary Blizzard
1887-1916 Robert Blizzard
1882 Leonard T Graham
1879 Robert William Batty
1877 H Barnes
1872 Mrs Jane Richardson
1870 T Richardson
1864-69 William Duffill
1858-59 Thomas Tindall
1846-55 Thomas Robinson
1834-40 Edward Mair
1826-31 William Mair
1823 John Stockdale
1814/15 Dorothy Mair
1802 John Mair

Moulders Arms
Wilbert Lane

A moulder was/is someone employed to make castings or moulds in a foundry and much of the regular trade in the Moulders Arms may well have been provided by the nearby Crosskill's Foundries in Eastgate and Mill Lane.

The Royal Commission on Historical Monuments survey suggested the Moulders building to be post-1860 however judging from evidence within the structure of the building

The Moulders Arms in Wilbert Lane, shown here in the 1950s has undergone many alterations since it was built circa 1830. Fortunately it remains relatively intact and offers a friendly atmosphere with a fine collection of pictures and bric-a-brac. (John Wyles)

and comparison of the 1852 and 1890 Ordnance Survey plans, it would seem probable that the building includes part of an earlier adjoining building. John Wood's plan of Beverley in 1828 appears to show a building on the same site. The census of 1881 recorded Henry Hurd as beer seller and grocer aged 66 with his wife, two sons, one granddaughter and his brother James a bill poster at the premises. By 1888 his son Thomas had taken over.

The Moulder's Arms has undergone a series of internal alterations and refurbishments that began as early as 1902,[170] but still provides a friendly atmosphere and has many interesting photographs, illustrations and bric-a-brac making it well worth a visit.

---

[169] DoE serial No.10/89/50.
[170] BOBE/6, 1902-23 for owner George Pape. East Riding of Yorkshire Council Archives.

SELECT VICTUALLERS
1987 Mary Wardale
1967 A Kerrison
1965 Cyril Dean
1955 H Gillyon
1943 F M Archer
1939 George Herbert Sheperdson
1937 William Scott
1915-30 Dunkley Rance
1922 Albert Border
1892-1916 Horatio Thomas Holmes
1889 Thomas Hurd
1879-82 Henry Hurd
1867-72 Wm Beautiman

Nag's Head
Grovehill
Also known as the Grovehill Tavern.

In a survey of 1806 showing occupiers of land within the estate of Beverley Corporation Mr H. Harrison was listed paying rent for *"ground and dock, near the lock"*, he paid 6s a year.[171]

Henry Harrison was an early victualler at the pub, one of many simply known as *"by the sign of the board"*, which became known as the Nag's Head.

When a pub was noted *"by the sign of the board"*, this referred to the sign or board displayed at the front of a pub that often contained a pictorial representation of the name of the pub. Innkeepers had been compelled by law to show a sign of some kind since the days of Richard II.[172]

Not all of the patrons of inns and alehouses were literate and the simple signs were an easy way of telling the public that this was an alehouse or inn and suggesting its name. Some were carved representations or sculptures, others were paintings.

The pictorial and carved signs were of course open to interpretation and this may account for the slight variations in the references to pub names in trade directories for example where the Swan may be read as the *White* Swan, the Red Lion becomes simply the *Lion* or the simple Bell becomes the *Ye Olde Blue* Bell etc. It is also likely that an inn, which had yet to be named, was simply referred to as the *sign of the board* until its name had become known and the plain board was painted-up.

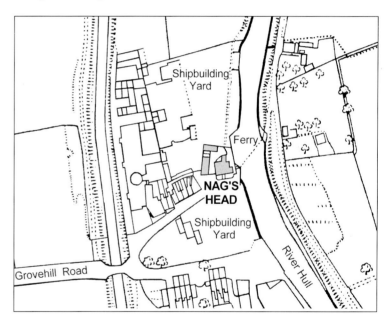

A map of the old Grovehill shipyards and ferry across the River Hull, which shows the location of the former Nag's Head pub.

---

[171] BCIV/4/3, East Riding of Yorkshire Council Archives.
[172] Richardson & Eberlein page 194.

Some victuallers of the Nag's Head also had the trade of ferrymen (1897) this would no doubt have been due to the close proximity of the old Grovehill Ferry. It was common for an inn to be at the site of a ferry and this was often the house of the ferryman and his family. Other victuallers at the pub had trades associated with the area e.g. a ships carpenter (1889) and even a ship owner (George Porter-1858/9). A document dated 19th November 1828 recorded:

"Particulars of Sale: ...Public house, shipyard, blacksmith's shop, 3 houses and 3 closes at Grovehill".[173]

The Nag's Head was situated opposite Cochrane's Shipyard and was almost the last building at the east end of Grovehill Road. The Nag's Head closed on 18th December 1908 and the licence was transferred to newly built premises in Holme Church Lane, called the Grovehill Hotel. Confusingly the Nags Head had been referred to as the Grovehill Tavern in some earlier directories, another example of a colloquial name being confused with the actual name.

SELECT VICTUALLERS
1897-1907 Henry Millett
1874-92 Thomas Harrison
1872 William Lundie
1869 William Lundie
1848-67 George Porter
1840-46 William Harrison
1823-34 Henry Harrison
1806 William Harrison

'Nellie's'
See the White Horse.

New Found Out
Highgate?

Another remembrance from the *alleged* journals of George Armstrong in which he wrote *"New Found Out was a beerhouse at the south east corner of Highgate (this was 30 years ago)"*. It is likely that Armstrong was writing from 1885 to 1917, this would suggest the New Found Out was open for business circa 1855. No beerhouses can be found in the nearest available directories, but this does not suggest there was not a beerhouse on the site. It was common for beerhouses to come and go within a matter of years and never be entered in the directories. It is listed here for the sake of completion and in the absence of any corroborating evidence.

Oddfellows Arms
Eastgate.
Also known as the Rooster?

No property was shown on the site of the Oddfellows Arms on John Wood's plan of Beverley of 1828 although other writers have suggested it was *"originally called The Rooster, which had its first licence in 1753"*.[174] The Royal Commission on Historic Monuments survey concluded the building was post 1780 and before 1860.
Many of Beverley's Oddfellows lodges of the friendly societies were formed around 1835-1840[175] and this would be a more likely date for the pub, which appeared in the trade directories for the first time around 1840.
George Armstrong allegedly recalled: *"F. Luden built place now used as Oddfellows Arms and carried on business as a druggist"*. A building plan in the East Riding of Yorkshire Council Archives dated March 1873 regarding alterations

[173] HUMAD ref. DDCV/15/213
[174] Inn Places of Beverley.
[175] David Neave.

The Oddfellows Arms was probably named in reference to the lodge of a Friendly Society that once met there. The former sign of the Oddfellows' can be seen in this photograph of 1987, which has sadly been replaced by a more modern interpretation. (Frank Pinfold)

and the addition of a new kitchen to the east of the old one at the Oddfellows Arms confirms F. Luden was the owner at that time.[176]

In 1881 the census recorded Charles Kirkham aged 31 as beerhouse keeper with his wife and two boarders at the pub. During a *"re-signing"* campaign by the *new* owner's John Smith's Brewery in 1988 the old signboard of the Oddfellows' depicting the banner of the Oddfellows Society was replaced by a modern sign showing what appeared to be three country yokels. Locals and the current lodge of Oddfellows, of whom the brewery either had no knowledge or had presumed defunct, met the new sign with predictable disdain.[177]

SELECT VICTUALLERS
1987 Trevor Cracknell
1915-39 Thomas Charles Puttnam
1913 E G Pape
1909 George Bell
1889-1905 John Warcup
1881 Charles Kirkham
1873-77 John Malton
1867 John Smith/ Robert Thomas Page
1851 Thomas Leng
1840 William/John Sheperdson

[176] BOBE/6/, 1873, East Riding of Yorkshire Council Archives.
[177] Hull Daily Mail 27.5.88

Old Oak Tree Inn
Dog & Duck lane.

The Oak Tree was recorded by name as a beerhouse in Dog & Duck Lane in Ward's Almanacs of the 1870s and the Beverley Echo of January 1885[178] ran an advertisement for:

"**STAFF ALE**, *The Leading Article,*
"At the OLD OAK TREE INN, John McGennis proprietor,
late staff sergeant 3rd East Yorkshire Regiment:
McGennis's STOUT is good no doubt In either wood or
bottle His famed STAFF ALE can never fail
To please a thirsty throttle!
-Devonshire Cider; 4d per bottle".

Later, in May of the same year another advertisement appeared to confirm the success of staff sergeant McGenniss's brew:

"THE FAR-FAMED STAFF ALE, 3d per pint;
Real Guinness's stout in Bottles;
Also, COMFORT, CIVILITY and CLEANLINESS
can be had at the-
OLD OAK TREE INN, John McGennis proprietor". (sic)

The census of 1881 showed victualler John McGennis to have lived in Keldgate with his family of six and not on the premises. The census also listed a property named *"Old Oak Tree Gatehouse"* in Dog & Duck Lane with the Bruce family of seven residents. This suggests that there had been a building or house in Dog & Duck Lane known as the Old Oak Tree which could have been the pub or simply that this was a common name in the area. From analysis of the census and comparison with the Ordnance Survey plans it is likely the pub was one of a pair of buildings on either side of a large arched entry on the north side of Dog & Duck Lane.

The Oak Tree beerhouse ceased to be recorded after 1895. Cook's directory of 1899 listed the Bruce family still resident and the next property vacant.

SELECT VICTUALLERS
1894 William Eason
1892-93 Mrs Jane Harrison
1891 Mrs Filby
1882-89 John McGennis
1879 Frederick Dean
1867-77 John Branton

Ox
Norwood
See the Durham Ox.

Pack Horse Inn
Market Place.

John Champion appeared as one of the first known innkeepers of the Pack Horse at the corner of Dyer Lane, in a directory of 1784. In his will in January 1808 he left *"two messuages on the east side of Market Place one being the Pack Horse Inn"* to his wife Hannah.[179]
The inn was "for sale" in the Hull Advertiser of 6th April 1821 and again 9th June 1837. George Armstrong allegedly recalled:

"the Pack Horse was a great centre for cock-fighting, it was kept by Ben Hood…it was rebuilt some 40 or 50 years ago, it previously having been a yellow coloured low-house".

---

[178] Beverley Local Studies Library.
[179] DDBC/35 Section Q/1, East Riding of Yorkshire Council Archives.
[180] Listed building description.

As Armstrong was writing circa 1895 this would suggest it was rebuilt circa 1850. The property adjoining the Pack Horse (No.37) was rebuilt in 1760[180] and this could suggest a date of building for the Pack Horse itself.

Although made redundant in 1925 when compensation of £1280 was paid to owners John Smith's Brewery of Tadcaster, it continued to be listed until 1928 in the trade directories.

The property was awarded Grade II listed building status in 1969[181] and has a *"heritage plaque"* on its wall containing brief details from its past. The imposing frontage overlooking Saturday Market is relatively unchanged from its days as an inn and currently the premises of an optician.

The sign of the Pack Horse was a common one and often denoted that the inn was a posting inn. In the case of Beverley's Pack Horse it can also be seen as a sign of the pub's age; as pack horses were one of the few means of transporting goods overland prior to the development and introduction of carts and wagons towards the end of the 17th Century. Before this all goods were transported by pack-horse or pulled on sleds.

By the same logic, a pub named the Coach & Horses or Waggon & Horses is unlikely to date from before the middle of the 17th Century.

The former Pack Horse buildings at the corner of Dyer Lane shown here in a photograph of May 2001.

A busy scene at the entrance to the former Pack Horse Inn Saturday Market around 1905. The building was rebuilt circa 1760 and may contain older remnants. (Beverley Local Studies Library)

[181] DoE serial No.9/331/69.

SELECT VICTUALLERS
1921-28 Joe Ellarby
1915-19 Charles Mathew Lister
1905 Mrs S James
1887-99 Enoch Welburn
1879-82 Henry Barnes
1877 H Whitton
1864-72 Jonathan Champion
1858-59 William Radge
1846-51 John Botterill
1840 Robert Terry
1831-34 Bainbridge Hood
1828/29 John Berriman
1823-26 Robert Clark
1814/15 Hannah Champion
1784-1807 John Champion

Plough
Flemingate.
See the Mariners Arms.

Prince of Wales (*Feathers*)
Eastgate.
Also known as the Three Merry Women?

In 1867 a man was fined for leaving a horse and cart outside the Prince of Wales beerhouse in Eastgate.[182] In a trade directory of 1867 two beerhouses were recorded in Eastgate, one of which was the Oddfellows Arms and the other must have been the Prince of Wales.
George Armstrong allegedly recalled:

> "*The Prince of Wales Feathers was a beershop in a house at the north side of Trinity Lane and Eastgate corner...this place was nicknamed the Three Merry Women.*" (sic)

As this beerhouse was recorded in the local press there can be little doubt of its existence, as for its alleged *nickname* - this could have been a reference to its sign or board outside that could have shown the three feathers, the emblem of the Prince of Wales.
If this location is correct this would suggest the current Chinese restaurant at the corner of Trinity Lane (No.57 Eastgate) was once a beerhouse, and would make it another of Beverley's Grade II listed buildings that was once a pub.[183] (This property is more likely to have been the *Rooster* mentioned in Inn Places of Beverley).

Prince's Feathers
Ladygate.
See the Custom House Vaults.

Push Inn
Saturday Market.

There had been a building of some description on this site since 1717, and it is known to have been rebuilt in 1755; it was formerly the apothecary and spirit merchant's shop of James Mowld Robinson.[184]
For its historic interest and surviving details it was made a Grade II listed building in 1950.[185] Jan Crowther wrote of Robinson in Beverley in Mid-Victorian Times:

> "*...and surely the most versatile of all – James Mould Robinson, who was a maltster, sold wines and spirits, brewed beer, both for consumption off and on the premises, dispensed medicines and operated as a surgeon, acted as an insurance agent, and sold corn. In 1851 Robinson lived over the shop, but by 1867 he had moved to a more elevated address in North Bar Without.*"

---

[182] Beverley in Mid Victorian Times, page 68.
[183] DoE serial No.10/42/87.
[184] Robert Barnard.

[185] DoE serial No.9/326/50.

Selling beer brewed on the premises, the apparently multi-purpose shop of Mowld-Robinson was a beer-shop of sorts and has been a pub therefore since at least 1851. A *"new dram shop"* was added in 1869.

The colloquial name "Push Inn" was allegedly taken from a door of the inn and has more recently has led to the name being recognised as its official title. During the 1980s the former wine vaults attached to the Push Inn became a wine bar known as the Grapes Cellars.

A spring 2001 view of the former apothecary and spirit merchants shop of James Mowld Robinson, now part of the Push Inn Saturday Market Place. The building dates from 1755, but has been radically altered in recent years.

During renovation in 1993 Beverley conservationists were on their guard and the following are extracts from the Hull Daily Mail, which followed the story:

"Conservationists are calling for safeguards to protect the character of a listed 18th century town pub earmarked for a £170,000 face-lift. Owners Bass Taverns want to re-do the interior and expand the building, incorporating an adjoining wine shop. The committee says existing windows in the present off-licence, which would be removed under the plans, should be retained, and that shutters and a door to the pub should not be replaced. They are also calling for the top floor of the building to stay in use instead of being closed off."[186]

"One of Beverley's most important buildings is to undergo major rebuilding work…conservationists have hit out at news that the 18th century Push Inn needs a new entrance to bring it into line with the latest safety regulations. The move comes after permission was granted for the Saturday Market pub to be extended into the shop next door. The alterations to the grade II listed building will involve taking out a window pane, repositioning a wooden pilaster and putting in a new three-panelled door and stone steps."[187]

The character of the building was greatly affected by the *"renovations"* and the chance to protect more of Beverley's invaluable and indeed irreplaceable architectural heritage was lost. Evidence that even listed building status is not enough protection against the modern developer. Thankfully the late Georgian bow window has survived all the alterations but a fine mid-18th Century building with a 19th Century pub interior has been changed beyond repair and whilst the Push Inn appears popular with the younger clientele, it now adds less than it could have to Beverley's charms.

[186] Hull Daily Mail 14.1.1993
[187] Hull Daily Mail 1.4.1993

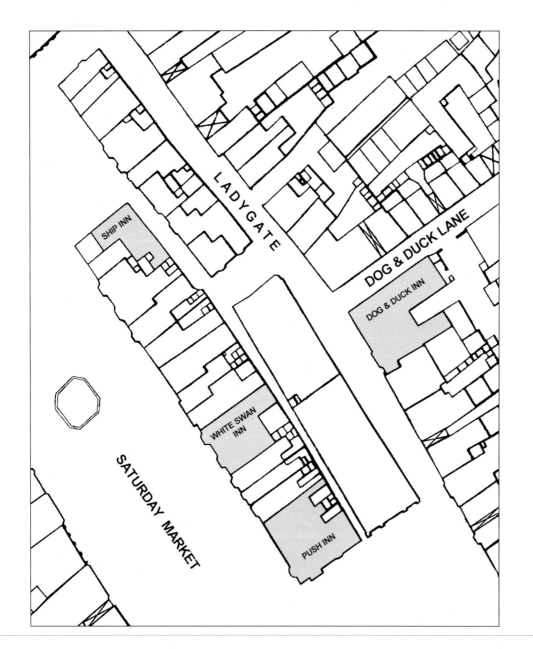

A map of the south end of Ladygate and the Dings circa 1890.

Queen's Head Inn
Wednesday Market.
Also known as the Hart?

An alehouse known as the *"Hart in Wednesday Market"* was mentioned in documents of the 16th Century[188] and this may have been an early reference to the property that became the Queen's Head.

Another more confident reference to the Queen's Head is contained in a bundle of documents relating to a *"messuage on the east side of Wednesday Market with three adjacent cottages on the north side of Cockpit Hill"*. The messuage was passed from Jane Agar widow, of Beverley to James Field in 1716.[189]

In the same bundle was a later description from 1811: *"messuage and three adjacent cottages one now converted into a* **brewhouse**".

In March 1802 Joseph Cook bequeathed *"the lease of the Queen's Head in Wednesday Market"* to his wife Jane and son John Pearson Cook.[190]

The 1851 Census recorded William Wilson aged 54, his wife, one daughter, a grand daughter, a visitor and one male servant present at the Queen's Head.

Originally the Queen's Head was a plain red-brick building similar to the remaining properties to its south. Sometime after 1899[191] it was rendered or *stuccoed* externally and a later photograph of circa 1920-25 shows it remained so for some time.

In February 1926 the council approved plans drawn by Beverley architects Whiteing & Reynolds on behalf of William Darley & Co. "to pull down and rebuild the front portion of the building". The whole of the building that fronted on to the Market was demolished to the wall of the old kitchen building at the rear (the plans noted that the *"kitchen and old buildings beyond"* were the only buildings that would remain).

The new construction, now gable-end to the street, was in the fashionable mock Tudor, imitation half-timbered design. The ground floor was in red-brick with stone blocking around the window and door. The glass in all the windows was imitation leaded diamond *"quarries"*. A central service area served a small front bar and rear smoke room, both entered via a long passage. The transformation was complete by September 1926.

It is difficult to ascertain whether the older buildings that were not demolished remain although the building was recorded as an 18th Century survivor in the survey of 1982 for the Royal Commission on Historical Monuments. A closer look may be required but sadly the ground floor has since been altered beyond recognition including the loss of the attractive lower section of the 1926 frontage.

[John Appleby, smith & victualler was listed in the 1791 directory in "Vizard Lane". In the 1792 directory he was listed as a smith & victualler in Wednesday Market; as the Queens Head is the only pub in the market place on an alley, is it possible he was a "whitesmith" making amongst other things, armour e.g. visors- also known as vizards- hence Vizard Lane? No other references are known re this lane name and it is of course possible that it was an error.]

SELECT VICTUALLERS
1987 Alan Harvie
1975 B P Clubley
1937-39 Charles Burks
1929 George Wild
1921 Charles Potter
1899-1916 Alfred Hardy
1887-97 Edmund Boddy
1879-82 James Steel
1867-72 John Turnbull
1848-64 William Wilson
1840-46 Thomas Clough
1804-15 James Parker
1802 Jane Cook
1800 Joseph Cook
1791-92 John Appleby
1716 James Field

---

[188] VCH.
[189] DDBC/15/147, East Riding of Yorkshire Council Archives.
[190] DDBC/15/180, East Riding of Yorkshire Council Archives.

[191] An illustration of circa 1899 (Britain in Old Photographs, page 18) shows it as plain brick.

A marvellous real photographic postcard of the original Queens Head building circa 1910, with what is likely to be former landlord Alfred Hardy at the door. This building was completely demolished for the construction of the current pub in 1926. This rendered front probably hid a very old property of the 17th Century, a sad loss.

The present Queens Head, shown here in a photograph of 1987. (Frank Pinfold)

Queens Head
Wednesday Market
Circa 1927

Kitchen

Back Entrance

Up

Smoke Room

Service

Counter

Bar

Passage

TINDALL LANE

WEDNESDAY MARKET

A plan of the "new" Queens Head as it appeared in 1927. Only the kitchen and rear buildings survived from the original buildings.

Railway Refreshment Rooms
Railway Station.
Also known as the Station.

The refreshment rooms of Beverley's Railway Station appear to have had a licensed bar since soon after it opened, circa 1846. The premises were listed simply as the Station in some directories.

The Refreshment Rooms at the station were listed as *new* in a trade directory of 1858 but had been recorded since 1855 at least and were clearly shown on the Ordnance Survey plan of 1852/3. The rooms are now lost within the modernised station building but were originally situated to the right of the main entrance hall.

The former rooms are now occupied by the excellent "Ceruttis 2" restaurant who maintain the buildings in good order.

SELECT VICTUALLERS
1912 F J Harrison
1882-95 Mrs Betsy J King
1869-77 Mrs McRobbie
1855-64 Francis Riggall

Railway Tavern
Wednesday Market

The Railway Tavern was, even by Beverley's standards, a small beerhouse that opened circa 1846, the same year as the newly constructed Railway Street itself was opened to the public.

Although the Railway Tavern continued to be listed in the trade directories until 1922 it was made redundant in 1918 when £1400 compensation was paid to the owners T. Linsley & Co of Hull.

Soon after this (circa 1924?) it was demolished for the widening of Eastgate corner, which had become too narrow for modern traffic.[192] Looking at the site today it would seem almost impossible to have fitted a pub in the space that is left. A photograph of the 1880s show it to have been a simple building (probably 17th Century) with gable-end to the market place. A typical beer-shop, bowed window frontage to Wednesday Market and a side door in Eastgate.

SELECT VICTUALLERS
1921-22 Joseph Hurst
1913-16 Charles Potter
1910 Harry Stubbs
1899-1909 George Benjamin Watson
1879-97 Mrs Eleanor Boulton
1848-75 Simpson Boulton
1846 Frederick Scott .

A view of the old "cross" in Wednesday Market that was removed in 1881. The photograph is looking south and shows the Railway Tavern at the corner of Eastgate to the left. The tavern was demolished in the late 1920s to widen the corner for modern traffic. (Beverley Local Studies Library)

[192] Nos.11 and 12 Wednesday Market were not listed after 1925 in the trade directories and No.10 was altered in 1924 (BOBE/6, 1924).

Red Lion

Toll Gavel.
See the Litchfield Hotel.

Reindeer

Wilbert Lane.

The Reindeer was a beerhouse on the north side of Wilbert Lane latterly being No.29.

It was not shown on Wood's plan of Beverley in 1828 but appears to be listed in the trade directories from around 1830, initially simply referred to as *"the sign of the Board"*. It may possibly have been purpose-built as a pub and was probably a product of the so-called "Beer House Act" of 1830.

Early in 1876 alterations took place for owners Hodgson & Gibson when a new *"shop window"* was added with *"red pilasters to each side"*.[193] In 1881 the census listed Edmond Boddy publican aged 38 and his wife Ann present at the pub. It held a beer-house licence until 1909 when it was made redundant. £782 was paid in compensation to the owners William Glossop & Bulay Ltd. on its closure.

Reindeer Yard (named with or after the pub) was adjacent to the property and survived until re-development of the area in the 1950s.[194]

SELECT VICTUALLERS
1908-09 Harold Thirsk
1899 Thomas Woodmansey
1897 James Bielby
1894 F Watts
1892-93 George Watts
1889 Joseph Jordan
1881-82 Edmond Boddy
1879 Wm Jackson
1858-72 Jemima Sneeston
1846-55 William Sneeston
1831-34 William Porte

[193] BOBE/6, 1875-64, East Riding of Yorkshire Council Archives.
[194] David Sherwood.

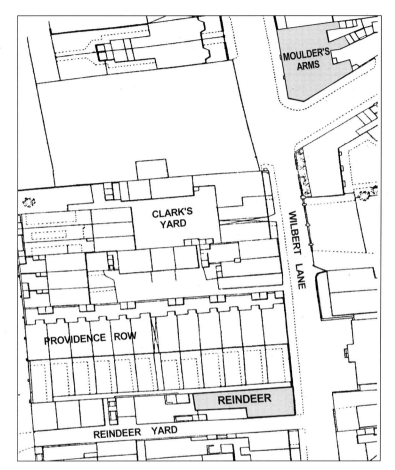

A map of circa 1890 showing part of Wilbert Lane and the former Reindeer Inn. The Reindeer', Reindeer Yard and most of the other buildings shown on the west side of Wilbert Lane were demolished in the 1950s for "redevelopment and improvements".

Rooster

Eastgate?
See the Oddfellows Arms.

Rose & Crown

York Road.
Also known as the Bull.

A feoffment dated 2nd March 1574 recorded the transfer of property *"in the occupation of Edward Thriske, cooper"* on the site of the present Rose & Crown. It recorded the transfer from *"Robert Fayrer, saddler to Stephen Smailes, tailor and wife Margaret: tenement called the **Bull**, and a garden and adjacent close lying without the north barres"*. It described the land as bounded by *North Barres* to the east, a field (*solum*) called the *Horse garden* to the west and private property to the north and south.[195]

Although the Rose & Crown was recorded in error as the *Crown & Anchor* on J Wood's plan of 1828 the property had been known as the Rose & Crown since at least 1800.

The large amount of rooms and the stabling attached to the inn were often used for the accommodation of racehorses and their owners whilst at the Beverley Races and hunters out on the West Woods. Many horses and pony sales took place in its yards.[196]

The following advertisement appeared in the Hull Rockingham 28th January 1815:

> *"**CAPITAL INN**, at **BEVERLEY**.*
> *To be SOLD or LET,*
> *All that Capital, Old-established, and Well-accustomed INN, at Beverley, in the county of York, called the Rose & Crown, now occupied by Mr. John Skelton.*
> *This is one of the principal Inns in Beverley, and is not only eligibly situated for Business in general, but particularly for the Quarter Sessions, Races, and Fairs, at which public times it does the principal Business. The greatest part of the House, Stables, and Buildings are new built, and the whole premises are in excellent Repair, and in every respect convenient and adapted for an Inn.*
> *Immediate possession may be had, and the person who buys or takes the Inn, will be required to purchase the FURNITURE, STOCK of LIQUORS, BREWING VESSELS, &c at a fair valuation.*
> *Further particulars may be had on application to Mr. Robt. Skelton, of Newstead Grange, near Malton; to Mr. Joseph Hall, of Beverley; or Mr. Samuel Bland, of Beverley; or to Messrs. Hall & Cambell, Solicitors, Beverley, Dec. 28, 1814."* (sic)

The Eastern Counties Herald of 18th November 1841[197] recorded *"Rose & Crown To Let with brew-house"*.

Later in the Census of 1851 James Skelton aged 70, his wife, one daughter, one son, two female house servants, one male outdoor servant and a single guest were recorded at the inn, which was again *"for sale"* in the Hull Advertiser of 25th February 1853.

The following notice appeared in the Beverley Guardian in December 1861:

> *"**TO BE SOLD** BY PRIVATE CONTRACT, all that extensive and well-accustomed INN, "The ROSE AND CROWN." situate without North Bar, BEVERLEY, near to the East Riding Sessions House, and adjoining the BEVERLEY WESTWOOD. Having Stabling and Loose Boxes for upwards of Eighty Horses, suitable for Race Horses, Hunters, &c.; Coach Houses, Sheds, Stack and Fold Yards, and a superior domestic Garden, well situated for Building purposes. The Property is Freehold, the situation excellent, and presents a very favorable opportunity for conducting a large and profitable business. For further particulars apply to Mr. ROBERT SKELTON, No.6, St. Mary's Terrace".* (sic)

---

[195] HUMAD.
[196] Jan Crowther.
[197] Robert Barnard.

Many pubs had their own spirit bottles made for use in their off-sales departments, known as pub flasks. This is an example from the Rose & Crown and dates from around 1900.

The present Rose & Crown, a 1931 structure that may incorporate earlier buildings possibly of the 17th Century.

The Rose & Crown's original address was York Road but it was drastically altered and re-fronted in 1931[198] for Darley & Co. in the style we see it today facing North Bar Without. Because of its stylish design it has become another of Beverley's Grade II listed pub buildings[199] although its listed building description appears to suggest it is older than it actually is. The plans for the redesign of the pub were approved in the winter of 1930 and in their letters to the Beverley Corporation the architects stated:

"as you will see from the plans we are pulling down the front and rear [east and west] portion of the premises and altering the centre portion. The heights of the floors etc. remain as at present."

The work was completed in June/July 1931.
The Rose & Crown's sign was described in 1939 as:

"Royal in character, first used in the time of Henry the Eighth. The White Rose of York, we observe, is surmounted by the Crown of England. It has been painted with artistic taste. At the end, hung on ironwork, is a luxurious bunch of grapes; the emblem denoting excellent wine is here sold".[200]

This article was written in 1939 and describes an inn-sign that was then probably only a few years old. A postcard view of the Rose & Crown of circa 1930 shows it had no signboard at that date and earlier (circa 1900) photograph shows it had none at that time also.

[198] BOBE/6, 1930-30. "New front etc. for Rose & Crown, York Road". East Riding of Yorkshire Council Archives.
[199] DoE serial No.9/239/87.

[200] Rambler, see bibliography.

A peaceful view of the junction of York Road and North Bar Without, now one of Beverley's busiest intersections. The view is looking west towards the Westwood and shows the original Rose & Crown pub. The pub was altered in 1931 when the small corner buildings became the present car park but the tall buildings were incorporated into the new structure. (Frank Farnsworth)

SELECT VICTUALLERS
1987 Robert Dawson
1929-65 Frederick Leach
1921 Edwin Sanderson
1897-1916 Robert Sanderson
1882-92 George Bodger
1877-79 William Shaw
1869-72 George Whitton
1858-67 John Holmes
1814-55 James Skelton
1791 John Fletcher
1574 Edward Thriske

1937-39 John William Dean
1921-29 Herbert William Castle
1915-16 Thomas Milner
1899-1905 Mrs L Franks
1892-97 Joseph Franks
1879-89 Aaron Sheperdson
1872 Robert Sanderson
1867 William Warkup
1864 Edward Milner

Royal Oak
Cartwright Lane.

The Royal Oak is a former beer-house that has been known colloquially as the *"Drum & Monkey"* for various obscure reasons. Possibly after the lane, which runs to its north (now Grosvenor Place) that was known as Drum and Monkey Lane in the 1800s. Allegedly the drummer from the band of the old Picture Playhouse lived there.[201]

The name of the Royal Oak may have been a reference to the nearby Westwood however the *"Royal Oak Lodge"* of the Oddfellows friendly society was formed in 1867 and there may have been a connection.

The census of 1881 listed Aaron Sheperdson as a beerhouse keeper and night watchman aged 66, at the pub with his two sons and a boarder.

The property underwent minor alterations in 1901[202] but retains much of its character.

The Royal Oak in Cartwright Lane, shown here in May 2001. The Royal Oak was probably built circa 1850 and is relatively unspoilt externally, probably due to its secluded location.

SELECT VICTUALLERS
1987 Jim Calvert
1975 K Lowe
1955-67 J W Ashman

[201] David Sherwood.
[202] BOBE/6, 1901-26. East Riding of Yorkshire Council Archives.

Royal Oak

North Bar Without.

This pub was recorded by name only once in 1831 but there were several beer retailers in North Bar Without that are as yet unaccounted for and it is likely the alehouse had been open some years prior (see *Strays*). It is highly likely that North Bar Without would have had a number of alehouses as horse and other fairs had been held there for centuries.

This may have been its first *official* listing after the beer-house act of 1830, which required licensing for the smaller houses. It ceased to be listed after 1840 and by 1864 the current Royal Oak in Cartwright Lane was open for business.

SELECT VICTUALLERS
1840 Mary Dawson
1831-34 John Dawson

Royal Standard Inn

North Bar Within.
Also known as the Boot and the Turf Inn.

The Census of 1851 recorded William *Cooms* (sic) aged 66, his wife and a daughter at a small small beerhouse then known as the Boot, but by 1858 the name had changed to the Turf Inn that was recorded as *new* in a trade directory of that year. The location of the pub, directly next door to the larger King's Arms, probably meant that it was frequented by the working classes whilst their *superiors* visited its larger neighbour. Its latter names suggest it may have been a place where you could have a wager on the races.

When David Steels took over in the 1870s it appears that he changed the name to the Royal Standard. In 1875 the Royal Standard lodge of the Independent Order of British Workmen was formed. This was a friendly society that may have met at the pub and may consequently have been a reason for the re-naming.

It was also in this year that a new *"Dram Shop window"* was added[203], the exterior details of which survive today.

The property is a Grade II listed building. The description given by the Department of The Environment in 1969 suggested that the building is possibly of the 17th Century and timber-framed, having been re-fronted in the 18th Century.[204] David Neave writing in the revised Pevsner also suggests that some of the properties on this row were re-fronted in the 1730s [Nos. 32-36 were refronted in 1736 by carpenter & joiner Peter Duke].[205] It is almost certain that the front of this unassuming pub hides a timber-framed building of the 17th Century. Due to its compact size it has limited scope for alteration and has managed to retain one of the more traditional front rooms (the former dram shop) of Beverley's pubs, which actually has the feel of a *real* pub and is worth a visit.

Coombs Yard still runs to the south of the block and is a reference to the well known former victualler of the pub during the 19th Century.

SELECT VICTUALLERS
1987 Ken Wild
1955-75 G A Wild
1899-1939 Thomas Charles Winsom
1897 Abraham Liversidge
1892 J Jordan
1879-89 David Steels
1864-72 Thomas Green
1858-59 William Boyes
1814-55 William Coombs

[203] BOBE/6/,1875-65 East Riding of Yorkshire Council Archives
[204] DoE serial No.9/234/69.
[205] Listed building descriptions.

Tucked in next to the imposing Kings Arms the stuccoed front of the Royal Standard looks very similar to the original Queens Head (see fig.73) and the same craftsmen may have carried out the work. The front hides a 17th Century timber-framed core.

Sanctuary

Lincoln Way.
See the Lincoln Arms.

Scottish Soldier

Highfield Road.
See the Eager Beaver.

Ship Inn

Market Place (Sow Hill).

In March 1756 the corporation granted a lease to:

> *"Luke Williamson innholder for a messuage on the south side of Sow Hill, [the] northernmost house in a row called the Dings in Saturday Market and the Swine Stye on the east side of Common Midden' belonging to the Shambles"*[206] (A midden was a dung-hill).

This appears to be the earliest reference to the Ship Inn, which was probably built in the 1750s.[207]
Francis Riggall aged 43 was recorded as a brewing victualler and retailer of wine and beer at the inn, in the census of 1851 (also present were his wife, a visitor and one female house servant). The Ship Inn was later owned by brewers Robert Stephenson & Son, of the Golden Ball Brewery in Toll Gavel[208] and held a full licence for the sale of wines and spirits as well as beer.
In the census of 1881 John Hall aged 28 was listed as innkeeper, with his young wife and five children with one domestic servant present at the inn.

---

[206] DDBC/16/178, East Riding of Yorkshire Council Archives.
[207] Pevsner page 306.
[208] Robert Barnard.

It ceased to be listed as a pub in 1915 having been made redundant in 1914 when £600 was paid in compensation to the owner Robert Ranby Stephenson. The *Rambler*, writing in 1939 noted:

> *"The Ship, on Sow Hill, was at one time signified by a hanging sign in wrought ironwork".* [209]

The fabric of the building still exists but is hard to distinguish as a pub as its former entrances have been removed. A side door to the former fish shambles is still visible in the passage to its east, but much rendering and moving of windows seems to have taken place when the building was restored and re-roofed in 1975. This included the complete removal of its main entrance to the Market Place, which was replaced by a matching window. It is still possible to imagine the appearance of the Ship; its five-bay frontage was almost symmetrical and the former door would have been under the surviving *blind* window in the centre. Fortunately the building was declared a Grade II listed building in 1950 and this may have prevented more drastic alteration of its details. [210]

SELECT VICTUALLERS
1899-1915 Frederick Knight
1897 Michael Fitzpatrick
1892 R Ward
1887-89 Thomas Watson
1881-82 John Charles Hall
1877-79 Mrs Harriet Holsworth
1858-72 James Walker
1855 Francis Riggall junior
1814-51 Francis Riggall
1791 Thomas Atkinson
1784 Thomas Anderson
1756 Luke Williamson

This calm sunlit view of the north end of Saturday Market shows the former Ship Inn. Its appearance in 2001 cannot hide the symmetrical lines of the former inn, the central door has been replaced with a matching window but its five-bay front is still clear. It closed as a pub in 1914.

[209] See bibliography.
[210] DoE serial No.9/318/50.

Sloop Inn

Beck Side.

The Census of 1851 recorded James Baker beerhouse keeper, aged 60 and his two daughters at the Sloop Inn; a pub that took its name from a type of vessel that would have been in common use on the nearby Beverley Beck and River Hull.

The Hull Advertiser of 16th July 1852 recorded that a *"Mariner's Society meeting was held at the Sloop Inn"*.

The building has been altered on a number of occasions the first known being in 1896, and in 1906 when toilets were added on behalf of the Beverley branch of John Smith's Brewery.[211]

Because of its age and some remaining details the building enjoys Grade II listed building status.[212] In its description it is described as being of the 18th Century, which is confirmed by some architectural details including its front window casings which are flush with the exterior of the building and are therefore likely to be of the mid-1700s. To the rear of the property is a typical Yorkshire sliding-sash dormer window of the same period.

The simple clean lines and lack of unnecessary decoration, signs etc. make the Sloop one of Beverley's least pretentious and most attractive pubs. It is also another that appears to have retained its original name for at least two hundred years.

SELECT VICTUALLERS
1987 Graham Anderson
1965-75 Mrs F E Anderson
1955 Mrs G Newton
1939 John R Robinson
1916-29 Charles William Coleman
1915 Mrs Jessie Spence
1905 Samuel Bowser
1899 Henry Fortnam

1897 William Richard Bird
1892 G H Warcup
1887-89 George Hulland
1882 Arthur Pearson
1877-79 Samuel Bielby
1872 William Watson
1867-70 Samuel Bielby
1864 John Bainton
1858-59 Robert Turner
1828-55 James Baker
1806-26 William Lowther

The Sloop on the south side of Beckside, is the last original pub in a group that surrounded the end of the Beck. It dates from the middle of the 18th Century and is a Grade II listed building.

[211] BOBE/6, 1896-17 & BOBE/6, 1906-13. East Riding of Yorkshire Council Archives.
[212] DoE serial No.11/6/87.

Sow & Pigs
North Bar Within?

Rambler, *"an old time scribe"* wrote of Beverley's signboards in The Announcer in 1939. He recalled:

> *"Standing on what is now a portion of St. Mary's Church Yard, and adjoining Dead Lane (this lane was absorbed onto neighbouring property many years ago) was the tavern known as the Sow & Pigs."*

Curiously, this same description was previously used by George Armstrong in his alleged reminiscences and has since been repeated in articles in the Beverley Guardian although none make the source of the information clear. Dead Lane ran along the east side of St Mary's Churchyard[213] and it is difficult to see how this could have been referred to as North Bar Within, however there were at least four buildings shown on the 1852 Ordnance Survey plan at the south end of "Dead Lane". One had been shown on Hick's plan of 1811[214] and two by Wood's plan of 1828 but by the time of the 1890 Ordnance Survey plan they were gone. It is possible that one of them may have been the alleged Sow & Pigs beerhouse, however no corroborating evidence has been found for either story and the Sow & Pigs is recorded here for the sake of completion only.

Spotted Cow
Eastgate?

George Armstrong allegedly recalled *"The first beerhouse in Beverley was the Spotted Cow in Eastgate"*. This may suggest the Spotted Cow in Wednesday Market was originally situated in Eastgate although there is no known corroborating evidence for this suggestion.

Spotted Cow
Wednesday Market.
See the Tim Bobbin.

The Spotted Cow was a beer-house situated within and probably at the rear of the butcher's that shared the site. Many if not all of the former beer-retailers listed at the pub also had the trade of butcher.
The first known illustration is of circa 1845[215] but is hard to locate in the trade directories until circa 1867. It closed as a pub circa 1937 but it is pleasing to note the property remains a butcher's today and is a Grade II listed building.[216] In its description it is suggested to be of the 18th Century. Photographs of circa 1920 show the pub with a large Worthington Ales signboard across its roof in direct competition with the Queens Head opposite that had an identically situated Darley's Ales signboard. Certainly a place you could have a *"pie and a pint"*!

SELECT VICTUALLERS
1936 George Rawson
1929-33 Herbert Pearce Duffield
1899-1925 Benjamin Lee Ramshaw
1897 Thomas William Finch
1877-92 Robert Sanderson
1874 Robert Spink
1867 William Rose

Station
Railway Station.
See the Railway Refreshment Rooms.

---

[213] VCH page 171.
[214] Ref. BC/IV/4/4. East Rididng of Yorkshire Council Archives.
[215] Image No.37 in Old Beverley.

[216] DoE serial No.10/403/69.

This picture postcard view shows the north side of Wednesday Market circa 1920. On the left is the former Spotted Cow beer-house (now Ye Olde Pork Shoppe) directly opposite its main competitor, the Queens Head.

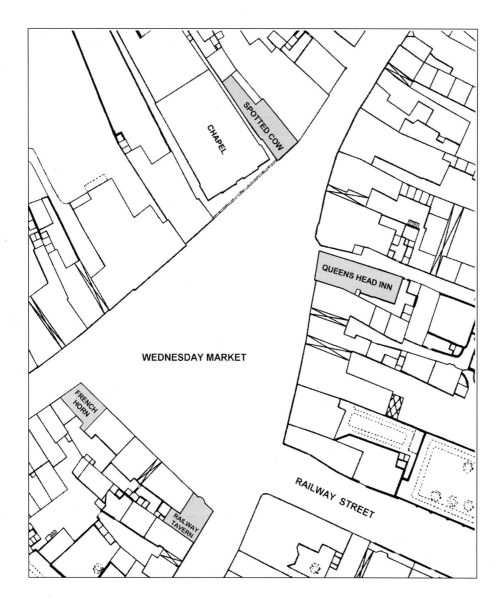

CHAPEL

SPOTTED COW

QUEENS HEAD INN

WEDNESDAY MARKET

FRENCH HORN

RAILWAY TAVERN

RAILWAY STREET

A map based on the 1890 Ordnance Survey plan giving the locations of the lost pubs of Wednesday Market and the surviving Queens Head. The shown location of the French Horn is the most probable of many suggested sites none of which have yet been conclusively confirmed.

Sun Inn

Flemingate.
Also Known as the Tabard (?) and the Tap & Spile.

The architectural and archaeological study of Beverley by the Royal Commission on Historical Monuments concluded that *"none of the surviving timber-framed buildings in Beverley appear to date from before 1400"*. This would seem to suggest an earliest *possible* date for the building that became the Sun Inn as circa 1400-1500.

David Neave writing in the revised "Pevsner" states simply *"The Sun Inn has a jettied front with brick-filled studding to the first floor, possibly of 16th-17th Century"*. Ivan and Elisabeth Hall suggested in Historic Beverley *"that until about 1660 the typical Beverley house was of half-timber and of very modest scale, often enough "two low rooms and two garrets beneath the thatched roof"*. It is clear that the precise dating of the structure is difficult without the benefit of accompanying evidence in the form of plans or deeds etc. It would seem that physical evidence "on the ground" has therefore been the basis for the present estimates of the age of the Sun Inn. For example, one indicator that could be used is that the projecting first floor joists appear to be laid on edge rather than flat. This was a practice not common until well into the 17th Century[217] and would push the estimated earliest possible date forward to at least 1600.

It is obvious that the extant building is almost certainly the original structure with later alterations. It seems likely that it would originally have been home to more than one family or trade. The timber frame showing through on the eastern end of the first floor has had its original *wattle and daub* in-fill replaced with herringbone brickwork, probably during the 18th Century when it was first fashionable to do so.[218] The vast majority of the timber-frame of the building is concealed externally by rendering although it is still evident that the ground floor has been built-out to square off the overhang of the jetty above.

It is likely that the Sun Inn was originally known as the Tabard, mentioned in the 16th Century in documents relating to the granting of Minster lands. It was referred to in French as *Le Taborre* in connection with three tenements in Eastgate *"which fell to the inn at the sign of The Tabard"*.[219] The Sun Inn had originally been three separate dwellings and falls within Minster lands, which suggests the two were one and the same.

The Census of 1851 recorded Bartholomew Stamford widower innkeeper and joiner aged 38, his daughter and his sister who was housekeeper at the Sun Inn, present at the time of the survey.

The following appeared in the Beverley Guardian, May 18th 1872:

*"**A PUBLICAN FINED***

At the Guildhall on Thursday, before the Mayor and J. Brigham, Esq., George Wiles, landlord of the Sun Inn, Fleming Gate was charged with keeping a disorderly house. Evidence was given to show that on Saturday afternoon last persons in a state of drunkenness were fighting in the defendant's house and yard, and that one or more of them were subsequently served by the defendant with drink. The case was reported to Supt. Knight, who visited the house in the evening and found fiddling and dancing in a front room in which were 60 or 70 people, including four prostitutes. Defendant's answer to the charge was that he did not know that he had done wrong and that he had nothing to say. With regard to what the Superintendent had said, he did not know the girls were prostitutes.- Sergeant Steel said he had repeatedly cautioned the defendant and also his wife against having prostitutes in the house.- Mr Shepherd, the magistrates' clerk, said that if the case was proved there were three

---

[217] Trudy West (see bibliography).
[218] Ivan and Elizabeth Hall noted *"In the later 14th century, brick ... might also in-fill the panels of a timber-framed building, set herring-bone fashion rather than in horizontal courses, as can still be observed in the outer wall of the Tap and*

Spile public house (formerly the Sun Inn) near the end of Friars Lane Beverley Friary" (Historic Beverley Page 41).
[219] George Dickinson, writing in the Beverley Advertiser.

A photograph of the enlarged Sun Inn from the 1920s, following its purchase by the Hull Brewery Co. Ltd. Note the traditional inn-sign and the original timber framing with later herringbone brick infill.

separate offences in it, viz., that of wilfully allowing drunkenness in his house, that of permitting gambling in his house (P.C. Haldenby having stated that he saw men playing at dominoes in the tap-room), and that of allowing persons of notoriously bad character to assemble in the house. Defendant was further informed that, for the first offence, he was liable to a penalty of £5, for a second a penalty of £10, and for a third a penalty of £50, and to forfeit his licence. The Mayor said the case was a bad one, and fined the defendant £3. And the costs, which were 18s 6d more". (sic)

The Yard to the north of the Sun Inn was known as Sun Inn Yard and appeared by name in the 1881 census.

In 1905 the Sun Inn had the first of many 20th Century alterations; owner Robert Ranby Stephenson of the Golden Ball Brewery converted the former pantry, scullery and coal-house into one large kitchen at the rear of the pub. A new scullery, pantry and coal-house were built in Sun Inn Yard to replace those lost. Upstairs, formerly one large "chamber", two bedrooms were created and fitted with sliding sash dormer windows.[220] Sadly, later less sympathetic alterations were to alter the interior of the building beyond recognition.

More recently the Sun Inn was taken over and much to the annoyance of almost everyone but the brewery, its long-standing name was removed. The Hull Daily Mail reported:

"A furore over proposals to change the name of Beverley's oldest pub was stepped up this week as councillors joined the row. The 16th Century Sun Inn would be changed to the Tap & Spile if owner Pubmaster continues with its plan, which also includes alterations as part of a £100,000

A real photographic postcard view of the Sun Inn from 1905 when the road opposite was being widened. Note the original Beer-shop entrance marked as the "Sun Inn Wine & Spirit Stores", later (circa 1910) to be concealed by the existing larger window.

[220] BOBE/6, 1905-9, East Riding of Yorkshire Council Archives.

renovation scheme".[221] And again "...the conservationists are urging Beverley Borough Council to refuse permission for signs bearing the new name to be erected outside the Flemingate building, which dates back to 1540 and is said to be haunted..."[222]

Nevertheless the Sun Inn re-opened as the Tap & Spile 28th September 1994. Following a change in opinion the inn has happily reverted to its former name and from December 2000 was once more known as the Sun Inn.

The Sun has been a Grade II listed building[223] since 1969 but this has not prevented what could be described as the systematic destruction of most of its interior in the ensuing decades. The only possible benefit of these alterations is that they have revealed the skeleton of the building and confirm its antiquity.

SELECT VICTUALLERS
1987 Brian Hardy
1965-75 J Gray
1939-55 George Redfern
1937 Alfred George Hirst
1929 William Henry Simms
1921 Samuel Nicholson
1915 William Goodall
1905 Harry King
1899 William Smith
1892-97 Michael G Thompson
1887-89 John Welburn
1877-82 Smith Welburn
1870-72 George Wiles
1864-69 Robert Arnott
1858-59 Thomas Stanley
1846-55 Bartholomew Stamford
1840 Nancy Stamford
1823-34 William Stamford
1814/15 Thomas Greenough
1791-1806 Francis Needham

Swan
Within the north bar.
See the White Swan.

An inn known as the Swan was mentioned *"within the north bar"* in the 16th Century[224] and may have been the property that became the Wheatsheaf, the Royal Standard or more likely the White Swan Inn that was known to have been within the dings and therefore within the bar.

Tabard
Eastgate.
See the Sun Inn.

Talbot
Highgate.

The Talbot was an alehouse mentioned in a 17th Century corporation lease granted to *"William Johnson for two shops on the south side, and one shop on the north side of an inn called the Talbot on the east of Highgate"* dated 2nd April 1645.[225]

It was mentioned again in the 18th Century in another lease dated 27th September 1766; *"John Anderson and wife Elizabeth to Hannah Whiting of Beverley Parks widow for £180 in all...now a public house called the Talbot"*.[226]

The Talbot may later have been known as the Black Swan or the French Horn. The French Horn was probably a hunting reference, as was the Talbot; a type of hunting dog.

---

[221] 5th August 1994.
[222] 21st July 1994.
[223] DoE serial No.10/48/69.

[224] VCH page 87.
[225] HUMAD
[226] HUMAD ref. DDCV/15/357

Tally Ho'
Norwood.

Another alleged reminiscence from George Armstrong's journal. In it he stated that the Tally Ho was "*now a pork shop next to Dr Calvert's…once occupied by T Marshall, chemist*". Francis Calvert, surgeon and later a JP lived at *The Laurels*, approximately seven properties east of the Valiant Soldier. There was a butcher at No.6 Norwood in 1915 [*Armstrong was writing circa 1917*] and this could have been the site of the Tally-Ho, alas there are no other references to this pub and it is another mentioned here for the sake of completion only, unless you know otherwise?

Tanner's Arms
Keldgate.

A bundle of deeds relating to the Tanner's Arms are stored in the East Riding of Yorkshire Council Archives, the earliest dated 1820 described the property as "*a house, and six tenements in Hind's Place*". Later documents in the bundle show an abstract of title for William Parker Birkinshaw for the Tanner's Arms for the period 1853 to 1889.[227]
Several yards in the area may have been named after former victuallers of the Tanner's Arms; Cook's Yard was listed in the 1861 census, and was shown on later maps to have been on the northern side of Keldgate, to the west of its junction with Lairgate. Pickard's Yard was listed in the 1861 census and was also to be found on Keldgate[228] (Cook's 1899 trade directory listed Pickard's Yard to the immediate west of Hind's Yard, almost at the junction of Lairgate, and Edmund Pickard was probably the first known victualler of the Tanner's Arms).

William Farrer, joiner and builder built the Tanner's Arms circa 1820. It was described in his will as a "*dwelling house with workshop, sheds, stable, gig-house and outbuildings*". Following his death in 1848 Joseph Hind purchased the property. Between 1848 and 1853 he built Hind's Place or Yard to the rear of the property, which consisted of twelve small cottages entered via an archway to the east of the pub. By 1867 it had its own small brewery, which may have been the former joiner's workshop and in 1889 brewers Glossop & Co. acquired the property as a small retail outlet.
The Tanner's Arms closed circa 1957 when its licence was transferred to the *new* Beehive across the road.[229]
During what was felt to be the unnecessary demolition of Nos.76 to 80 Keldgate circa 1970 the Tanner's Arms was lost along with an adjoining house and a former Wesleyan Mission Hall. In the wall of the former brewery building was a carved angel holding a shield bearing a stag's head that was rescued by a member of the Beverley Civic Society.
The Tanner's name was a probable reference to the trade of the first licensee and the majority of his customers who would no doubt have worked at the nearby tanneries. Fortunately high quality photographs of the buildings survive from the former Hull Brewery archives and give an accurate record of the area.
(*The majority of the information on the Tanner's Arms came from an article by David Neave for the Beverley Civic Society*).

SELECT VICTUALLERS
1937-39 Mrs Annie E Gray
1930 Charles E Cheeseman
1929 Claude Todd
1926 Fred Hill
1922-25 Benjamin J Whinnerah
1913-21 Alfred Bentley
1899 Louis Caley
1894 Lucy Barker

---

[227] DDBC/15/451.
[228] David Sherwood.
[229] Inn Places of Beverley (no source)

A calm view of Keldgate in the mid-1920s; note the total lack of traffic. The Tanners Arms on the right of the picture was demolished along with the adjoining house and the former Wesleyan Chapel to its west in 1970. Note also, the entrance to Hind's Yard on the right.

A MAP of circa 1890 showing the junction of Keldgate and Lairgate. The Tanners Arms is clearly shown at the entrance to Hind's Yard on the bottom right, also the original Beehive Inn on the west side of Lairgate to the left.

1892-93 Mrs Lucy Cook
1874-89 John Cook
1867-72 Richard Lamb
1860-64 William Thompson
1858-59 James Abbott
1840 Edmund Pickard

Tap & Spile

Flemingate.
See the Sun Inn.

Telegraph Hotel

Trinity Lane.

The Telegraph Hotel was built in the 1840s (probably circa 1844) on the former gardens and nurseries of Mr Tindall. David Neave suggests in the revised Pevsner; *"Telegraph Hotel of the late 1840s. The grey facing bricks and wide pedimented doorcase were reused from the 1804 theatre in Lairgate"*.

The address of the Telegraph was originally (and correctly) recorded as Grovehill Lane, which at that time began at the junction with Trinity Lane. Later, possibly following the construction of Station Square, its address began to be recorded as Trinity Lane. The first section of Grovehill Lane had become separated from the rest by the *new* railway lines and it seems the small portion that was left then became known as part of Trinity Lane.

The Telegraph probably took its name from one of the many coaches that ran from Beverley, a trade that was challenged by the new railway station soon after the construction of the hotel.

During Nicholas Thrusk's thirty-year occupation of the Telegraph Hotel he often advertised its considerable facilities, for example in 1878:

"Under the patronage of H.R.H the Prince of Wales, The Duke of Cambridge, Lord Londesborough &c.
NICHOLAS THRUSK
COACH & CAB PROPRIETER
In thanking the public for their favours begs to state that he is enabled to supply Bridal Carriages, One and Two horse hearses, Mourning Coaches, Cabs, Gigs, Dog Carts, Omnibuses, Waggonettes and Post Horses to suit all classes. TELEGRAPH HOTEL, Beverley".[230] (sic)

The pub continues to trade and evidence of its coaching past can be seen from the later addition of an arched coach entrance at its eastern side.[231] Also worth a look is the old painted advertisement for Magnet Pale Ales on the front wall.

SELECT VICTUALLERS
1987 Albert Curtis
1965-75 J Anderson
1939 George Taylor
1937 Alex. Anderson
1929 George Taylor
1915-21 Misses B E & F M Sugden
1889-1905 Mrs Hannah Sugdon
1877-87 Nicholas Thrusk
1870-72 Mrs Elizabeth Thrusk
1855-69 Nicholas Thrusk
1848-51 Thomas Payne Johnson

This 1987 view of the Telegraph Hotel clearly shows the arched entrance to the former stables of Nicholas Thrusk, a former tenant. The pub is still popular with ardent locals but in an area of Beverley a little off the beaten track the pub is clearly at risk from speculative developers. (Frank Pinfold)

[230] John Ward's Beverley Almanac for 1878, Beverley Local Studies Library.
[231] Not shown on the 1853 Ordnance Survey Plans.

Three Merry Women

Eastgate.
See the Prince of Wales.

Tiger

Highgate.
See the Black Swan.

Tiger Inn

North Bar Within.

Early recorders of this inn often mis-spelt the name; the Hull Courant of 10th March 1759 recorded a meeting of the officers of the East Riding Militia at *"the Tyger Inn Beverley"*.

The Beverley Corporation Minute books of 3rd September 1804 recorded that the Corporation had no objection to *"Mrs Charter putting out signs in respect of the Tiger Inn"*.[232]

The signboard of the Tiger was hung from a "gallows style" structure that stretched across the footpath and out into the road. This long overhead beam was supported by upright posts and was the stopping point for coaches requiring a change of horses.

The name of the Tiger may possibly have come from the nickname given to the young lad, a liveried servant, whose duty it was to put-up the luggage and ride at the back of the carriage, known as the *Tiger*.[233]

The building itself is of circa 1740[234] but closed as an inn in 1847 when the name was transferred to the Tiger in Lairgate. It was recorded as *"the sign of the Tiger"* in the York Courant of 26th June 1770.[235]

This image, after an original by Luke Clennel, shows the former Tiger Inn on the west side of North Bar Within circa 1845. The building served its last as a pub in 1846/7 and has since been converted into shops.

[232] Beverley Corporation Minute Books page 88.
[233] Brewers Dictionary of Phrase & Fable.
[234] Pevsner, page 320.

[235] Hull Local Studies Library.

The building has been saved from the developers over the intervening years due to its continued commercial success as a series of shops. It takes little imagination to see it as an inn. For the complete history of the Tiger, one of Beverley's premier coaching inns, readers should refer to History of the Tiger written by John Markham in 1988 to which very little can be added.

SELECT VICTUALLERS
1823-46 Charles Greenwood
1814/15 Thomas Russell
1811 Jinsy Harrisson
1804 Mrs Charter
1791 William Charter
1770 Mrs Todd

It takes little imagination to remove the modern shops from the building that was once known as the Tiger Inn, one of Beverley's principal establishments. The elegant building, which survives on the west of North Bar Within is shown here in a photograph of May 2001.

Tiger Inn
Lairgate.
Also known as the Black Bull.

In December 1746 the Corporation granted a lease to: *"Peter Thompson joiner, a messuage called the Black Bull in Laregate and adjacent tenement on the south side of Minster Moorgate".*[236] The Black bull, *"with brewhouse"* was advertised to let in the Hull Advertiser in January 1820 (*"apply Mrs. Linward"*) and again in 1845.[237] It was probably following the latter sale that it changed its name to the Tiger following the closure of Beverley's most famous Tiger Inn in North Bar Within.

Farrah's Yard was listed in Lairgate near the Tiger Inn and may have been named after John Farrah who was victualler at the Black Bull in the 1840s.

The census of 1851 recorded Frederick Scott aged 59, his wife, one son and two lodgers present at the inn. In 1858 prostitute Fanny Turner was found fighting on the floor of the Black Bull with another woman. She was described in the press as *"a young lady of no enviable reputation".*[238]

During the 1860s and 1870s when the Bainton family held the inn it was noted in the trade directories to also have a *"shop"*. Whether this was an early *"off-sales"* or bottle and jug department, or another type of business altogether is not known.

The sign of the Bull was a common one but as this one was black it may have been a reference to a local coat of arms containing a black bull.

The Tiger Inn is now a Grade II listed building and is described in its listing as:

"Double pile building of early 19th Century [surely 18th Century] *origins, re-fronted in the 3rd quarter of the 19th Century,* [2nd quarter of the 20th Century] *probably by*

---

[236] DDBC/16/163, East Riding of Yorkshire Council Archives.
[237] Hull Advertiser, 28.3.1845.
[238] Beverley in Mid Victorian Times, page 70.

Elwell. Two storeys, brick, rendered below ground floor windows, with tile roof and applied half-timbering. Two windows of three lights flank gabled centre with barge-boards carved with vine leaves. The gable has two windows of two lights, below brackets carved with roses. Ground floor has two windows flanking a studded door. There are two ornamental rain waterheads at the end of the gable".[239]

The pub is certainly one of Beverley's most attractive and under the ownership of Darley & Co. it underwent a series of alterations beginning in 1912, which resulted in the impressive mock half timbering re-front of 1931 which it retains.[240] Although there appears to be confusion within its listed building description as to the age of the Tiger and its decoration, the evidence is quite clear and the core of the building would appear almost certainly to be of the first part of the 18th Century. The frontage was in fact designed by Hull architects Wheatley & Holdsworth (also the Rose & Crown of the same date) and fitted in 1931. At this point the interior was slightly altered and a small *"bottle & jug"* shop at the south end of the bar was removed. Sadly it was also in 1931 when all of the former stables and outbuildings were lost; the plans noted *"all of these outbuildings to be pulled down and cleared away"*.

The pub retains a long list of original features from the 1931 re-fit and before. Well worth a visit for more investigation and to note the almost unchanged layout, which gives a good reminder of how pubs *used* to feel.

SELECT VICTUALLERS
1987 David Foster
1975 K P Berry
1967 Stan Rayner
1965 T B Robson
1955 J H Hogarth
1939-43 George V Tunstall

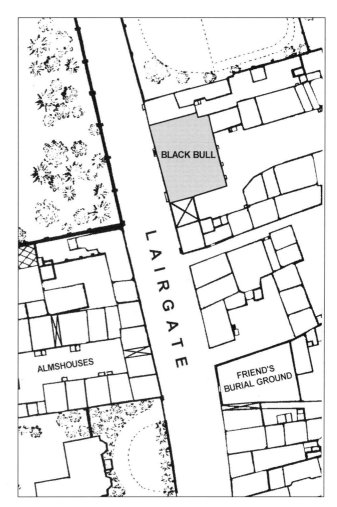

A map of circa 1890, which shows the location of the Black Bull Inn, now the Tiger Inn, Lairgate. Note the building at the south of what was originally an arched yard entrance, that was lost for the widening of the gateway in 1931. Sadly all the outbuildings and stables at the rear of the pub were also demolished at that time.

---

[239] DoE serial No.8/142/87.
[240] BOBE/6, 1912-10, BOBE/6, 1930-40a & BOBE/6, 1930-45. East Riding of Yorkshire Council Archives.

1937 Frederick George Harrison
1929 Joseph Brown
1921 Mrs Mary Brown
1897-1916 Joseph Brown
1892 E Voase
1879-89 Mrs Sarah Bainton
1867-72 John Bainton
1864 William Young
1858-59 William Lovell Jnr.
1848-55 Frederick Scott
1846 William Medcalf
1840 John Farrah
1814-34 Robert Watson
1784-1806 Peter Watson
1746 Peter Thompson

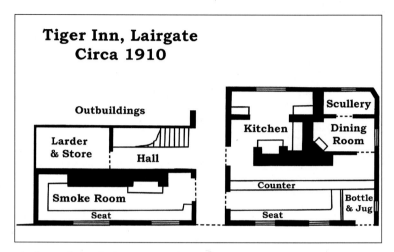

A floor-plan of circa 1910 showing the early layout of the Tiger Inn, that was only slightly altered in the works of 1931.

The impressive frontage of the Tiger Inn Lairgate, which is almost certainly Beverley's most intact 1930s pub. The Building was re-fronted and altered in 1931; note the side door to the right of the picture that was originally the entrance to the off-licence or "bottle & jug".

Tim Bobbin
Butcher Row.

This one-off listing was recorded in the trade directory of 1831 and may have lasted only a year or two. The so-called Beer House Act had been passed in 1830 and a mass of new licensed premises opened in the following years but many disappeared as quickly as they came.

Rambler, *an old time scribe* writing in 1939 suggested this was an early name for the Spotted Cow whose address was actually Wednesday Market but there is no known corroborating evidence to support his theory.[241]

SELECT VICTUALLERS
1831 William Padgett

Trafalgar
Molescroft.
See the Molescroft Inn.

Traveller's Rest
Beck side.

This beer-house appears to have started life as a marine store dealer's shop and may have begun to serve ale to its customers who would have been thirsty sailors etc. from the Beverley Beck. The Traveller's Rest was listed as *new* in an 1858 trade directory.

The yard that was situated next to the pub was known as Traveller's Rest Yard in the latter part of the 19th Century and survives as part of the building itself.

Long term residents at the pub were the Coates family from the 1860s to the 1890s. The 1881 census listed John Coates aged 52 as head of the household, an innkeeper and marine stores dealer. With him at the pub were his wife, five sons, four daughters, a female visitor and one boarder or lodger.

Extensive alterations were made in the winter of 1896 for owner Harry Glew at which point a new *"Club Room"* was added at the rear of the property, suggesting that the pub may have been used by one of Beverley's Friendly Societies[242] for their lodge meetings.

Old Flames of Beverley, originally the site of the Travellers Rest beerhouse. The beer-shop front is clear on the right of the building and to the left the shutter conceals what was once Travellers Rest Yard. The building closed as a pub in 1924 and was known to locals as Brentano's cycle shop and garage for many years.

[241] See bibliography.
[242] BOBE/6, 1896-21. East Riding of Yorkshire Council Archives.

The pub was made redundant in 1924 when £800 was paid in compensation to the owners T. Linsley & Co. of Hull following its closure.

It became a garage and cycle engineer shop known locally as Brentano's, which it remained for many years. "Old Flames" who supply reproduction fire surrounds etc. currently occupy the buildings and many architectural details and furnishings remain inside. The dimensions of the largely unaltered rooms and their layout give a good impression of a typical Victorian beerhouse; well worth a look even though they don't sell beer.

SELECT VICTUALLERS
1910-24 John Nevison Taylor
1899 John Hancock
1897 John Hunter
1894 T Coates
1892-93 Mrs Eliza Coates
1864-89 John Coates
1858-59 William Watson

Tudor Rose
Eastgate.

This property, long known simply as the Tudor Rose restaurant, also opened as pub in 1985 and allegedly incorporates timbering and windows from the Golden Ball pub that was in Toll Gavel.[243] The building has listed building status awarded in 1982[244] and in its description it is described as of the "mid-18th Century".

Turf Inn
North Bar Within.
See the Royal Standard.

Tyger Inn
North Bar Within
See the Tiger Inn.

Valiant Soldier
Norwood.
See the Cornerhouse.

Wheatsheaf
North Bar Within
See the Beaver.

White Horse Hotel
Hengate.
Also known as Nellie's.

Nellie's is an incredible survivor that is quite deservedly a Grade II *star* listed building[245] and probably one of the finest surviving examples of an intact 19th Century (very possibly earlier) pub interior in the north of England.

Dugdale (an emissary of Charles the second) allegedly wrote his pedigrees of families resident in Beverley and the East Riding from the White Horse in 1666.[246]

The property was described in a corporation lease to widow Susannah Sokill of Beverley dated August 1732 as:

"two messuages or tenements containing nine low rooms and twelve chambers being all covered with tiles, viz. all the front (except the gatestead) over the hall and barr and back part of the said gatestead with flat tiles, the remainder with pan tiles. And three stables covered with thatch, one court garth,

---

[243] Inn Places of Beverley (no sources)
[244] DoE serial No.10/396/82.
[245] DoE serial No.9/84/50.

[246] Rambler, see bibliography.

*Nellie's, or the White Horse is probably the finest example of an intact 19th Century pub interior in East Yorkshire and a Grade II **star** listed building. The shell of the building is of the 17th Century or earlier. If you haven't been, why not?* (Frank Pinfold)

two other little garths thereto adjoining on the south side of Hengate. Also one garden place adjoining on Silverlace Lane containing fifty-six yards in length and thirteen yards breadth."(sic)[247]

The Census of 1851 recorded Frances Burrell a widow aged 56, his two sons, two daughters, a sister, a grand daughter, a visitor, one male outdoor servant and one female house servant present at the White Horse.

In a later corporation lease of December 1862 to Francis Burrell it was described as:

"all that house or dwelling house in Hengate...used as an inn or public house and known by the name or sign of the White Horse with the stables, brewhouse, saddlers shop, yards and conveniences thereto adjoining. Also a cottage adjoining thereto on the west side."(sic)[248]

This later description shows how the pub had grown by this point and acquired buildings for the trade of the victualler. David Neave writing in the revised Pevsner guide suggests:

"The curving facade of Nos.18-24 [Hengate] suggests 17th Century or earlier timber-framing, brick fronted in the early 18th Century. The main section forms the White Horse Hotel, which retains a remarkable array of 19th Century public-house fixtures and fittings. Here also can be seen posts and brackets of a bressumer some two feet behind the later frontage."[249]

Local historian John Markham stated that:

"The White Horse property was owned by St.Mary's until 1928 when Francis Collinson (previously a tenant) bought it. He was succeeded by his daughter-Nellie whose name virtually supplanted its official title."

Samuel Smith's Brewery bought the White Horse from the Collinson family in 1976.

Nellie's gas lamps, narrow passages, small rooms and lack of exits have always been of concern to the authorities and the Hull Daily Mail reported in 1989 that the *"Police concerned with the level of safety at Nellie's called off an inspection following all clear from the council inspector"*. Fortunately these concerns have not caused too many alterations, however more recently a rather unnecessary and possibly ill-advised "eating area cum games room" has been added to the rear of the building. However, Nellie's remains an all-time favourite pub of the author. Every visit seems to result in another discovery about its history or to reveal another detail about its structure and internal details. It is difficult to recommend this pub highly enough – just go and see.

SELECT VICTUALLERS
1987 Bruce Westoby
1937-39 Mrs Elizabeth J Collinson
1892-1929 Francis Collinson
1848-89 Francis Burrell
1823-46 William Burrell
1806-15 Nathan Hart
1791-1805 Israel Marshall
1787 Robert Marshall
1770 Wm Berriman
1753 Thomas Berriman
1732 Susannah Sokill
1725 Mathew Remington
1715 John Watson
1708 William Chevey
1705 John Harpham

247 Ref. PE 1/47. Courtesy of Jan Crowther.
248 Ref. PE 1/204. Ibid.
249 Page 308.

White Lion
Location unknown

The council granted *"leave to Charles Tenyson, grocer, to put out a bow window in the house lately known by the Sign of the White Lyon"*, on the 4th April 1768.[250] Sadly the whereabouts of the pub are unknown but it is likely that this was simply an earlier name for one of the other *known* sites, possibly within the Dings.

White Swan Inn
Market Place.

Ivan and Elizabeth Hall's survey of Beverley's older properties suggested the former White Swan was built between 1740 and 1758.[251]

The 1851 Census recorded Michael Hind aged 66, his wife, one daughter, one son, a grand daughter, one female house servant and a visitor present at the inn.

The census of 1881 listed Matilda Harris *"joiner's wife"* as the head of the family aged 31 (her husband David Harris, listed as victualler from 1877-79, was not recorded). Also present were her four sons and four daughters all below the age of 12. David Neave writing of Saturday Market in the updated Pevsner said *"some good shop signs including... the figure of a white swan on No.23, a former inn"*. The sign is still in-situ (although a later replacement) on what is currently Michael Phillips jewellers shop.

The now well-known sign was described in 1939 as:

"a finely carved figure of this beautiful bird, round whose neck is decked a golden crown or chain- a mark of a first-class house of entertainment. These, as licensed premises, were closed some years ago."[252]

The present replacement swan has no ring of gold and is quite plain.

Although it continued to be listed in the trade directories until 1926 the White Swan had been made redundant in 1924 when compensation of £600 was paid to the owners the Hull Brewery Co. Ltd.

The building has been Grade II listed since 1969[253] but the frontage has been greatly altered since its days as a pub.

SELECT VICTUALLERS
1925-26 Walter Binks
1921 Charles Mathew Lister
1915-19 Frederick Curtis
1906 Mary Jane Emeny
1899 John Edward Hustler
1897 Charles Voase
1892 C Witherwick
1889 Charles Leader

An 1899 advertisement for the White Swan Hotel formerly of the Market Place, now a jewellers. Note "variety concerts every evening".

[250] Beverley Corporation Minute Books page 48.
[251] Historic Beverley page 6.
[252] Rambler, see bibliography.
[253] DoE serial No.9/323/69.

1887 George Leader
1882 Charles Kitchen
1877-79 David Harris
1872 Frederick Ward
1864-70 William Browsho'
1826-59 Michael Hind
1823 James Donaldson
1814/15 John Donaldson
1791-92 John Allison

Windmill Inn

Lairgate.
Also known as the Carpenter's Arms.

The former Carpenter's Arms was a beerhouse once owned by Mair & Clarke brewers of Wilbert Lane[254] that later became known as the Windmill Hotel. The change in title was recorded in the local press circa 1844.[255] However it continued to be recorded (e.g. in Ward's Almanac of 1874-1877 and 1894) as the Windmill Inn for some time.
Owners John Smith & Co. altered the property in the autumn of 1912.[256]
An 18th Century corner cupboard from the Windmill Hotel, Lairgate is preserved in the sitting room of No.8 St. John Street.[257]
Windmill Walk is now situated alongside the Windmill public house, and runs between Lairgate and Toll Gavel.

SELECT VICTUALLERS
1987 Alan Wilkinson
1975 Mrs Battersby
1955 J L Parker
1937-46 Albert Edward Johnson
1929-30 William Acred
1897-1921 John Acred
1894 Elizabeth Malton

The Windmill Inn tucked away in Lairgate was originally known as the Carpenters Arms. Its gable-end to the street configuration is a possible clue to its age and it is known to be early 18th Century.

1879-92 John Malton
1848-77 William Smith
1840-46 Hannah Brown
1834 Thomas Brown
1831 John Simpson
1828/29 William Ripon
1826 Thomas Dutton
1823 James Dutton
1806-15 Robert Scruton
1791 Robert Reveley

[254] Robert Barnard.
[255] David Sherwood.
[256] BOBE/6, 1912-17. East Riding of Yorkshire Council Archives.

[257] Beverley Civic Society.

Woolpack Inn

Westwood Road.
Also known as the Boy & Barrel.

Originally known as the Boy & Barrel, the history and development of this pub is on display inside the building. It states that it had been built as two cottages circa 1825/26 and became known as a pub circa 1831 [*probably following the Beer House Act of 1830*]. It also states it was renamed the Woolpack in 1840, however the Publican's Retail Spirit Licence recorded it as the Woolpack slightly earlier in 1837.

The Woolpack Inn, Westwood Road, shown here in a photograph taken on behalf of the Hull Brewery Co. Ltd. circa 1925. It was originally known as the Boy & Barrell and was built a hundred years earlier, circa 1825.

258 Courtesy of John Markham.

A Victorian advertisement for the Woolpack stated:

"the premises are commodious and favourably situated for carrying on a good business, being close to the principal entrance to the Westwood and some distance from other licensed houses."[258]

At that time it had its own brewhouse and a three-stalled stable to enable travellers to put up their horses. Some time later circa 1889, Richard Harrington sold the business to Cooper & Close, wine and spirit merchants of York. At that time the pub had a yard, brewhouse, stable, granary, washhouse and other buildings. In 1896 the Hull Brewery Co. leased the property and in 1936 bought the pub outright.

A photograph of circa 1927 from the former Hull Brewery archive shows the Woolpack very similar to how it appears today. Sadly a wonderful gas-lit glass globe bearing the Woolpack's name hung from an elegant bracket is no longer in place.

Writing of Beverley inn signs in 1939, the *Rambler* noted:

" The Wool Pack in Westwood Road, was the old emblem of a Wool Merchant. It is pleasing to write that the latter sign has in recent months been replaced. The new erection is a very imposing two sided painting depicting a merchant or merchants travelling in the country with horses laden with Wool Packs. This indeed is very striking evidence that a revival of the old-time inn signs is being revived."[259]

The Woolpack has Grade II listed building status that was awarded in 1987[260] and retains a very warm and welcoming atmosphere cherished by its locals.

SELECT VICTUALLERS
1987 Alan Glue
1975 A K Railton
1965-67 E S Boynton
1937-39 William T Richardson
1929 James Pearson
1916-21 Mrs Emma Hebden
1915 Mrs Ellen Hutchinson
1897-1905 David Steels
1892 R Allison
1858-89 Richard Harrington
1846-55 John Hutton
1837-40 John Widdall
1831-34 John Hutton

World's End
Keldgate?

Another of George Armstrong's alleged reminiscences, possibly a colloquial name for the Duke of York, of which he recalled *"Roebottom kept the World's End"*.

---

[259] See bibliography.
[260] DoE serial No.7/409/87.

Strays

Following the so-called Beer House Act of 1830 many small pubs sprang-up around England. From 1830 many new pub sites and names were listed in the trade directories. Many of the victuallers were mentioned by name only in the directories and inevitably moved on often within a year, leaving a long list of "stray" references that are impossibly difficult to place. They are listed here for the sake of completion in the absence of any further evidence.

Butcher Row
1867 – Jane Lundie, beer retailer
1864 – Thomas Stanley, beer retailer
1840 - William Wilkinson, beer retailer

Dyer Lane
1834 – Robert Skipper, beer retailer

Grovehill Lane
1840 – John Sheperdson, beer retailer

Highgate
1872- Miss Mary Jane Riggall, beer retailer

Hull Road
1834 – Samuel Sunman, beer retailer

Keldgate
1834 – James Robinson, beer retailer

Lairgate
1858-59 - Thomas Drewry, beer retailer
1855 - John Ramshaw, beer retailer

Market Place
1864 - Thomas Hood, beer retailer
1867 - John Warcup, beer retailer

Mill Lane
1874 -1877 G Petch, beerhouse
1894 - Eliza Cumberland, beerhouse

Minster Moorgate
1840 – Hannah Duncan, beer retailer
1834 – Peter Duncum, beer retailer

North Bar Within
1864-67 - Ann Andrews, beer retailer
1834 – John Andrew, beer retailer

North Bar Without
1834 – William Witty, beer retailer

Norwood
1867 – Thomas Dent, beer retailer
1840 – George Lister, beer retailer

Toll Gavel
1814/15 – Pearson Newton, beer retailer

Historical chronology

The following are a series of references relating to the inns of Beverley compiled from secondary sources and based in part on a chronology first produced by Chris Ketchell as "Beverley's Pubs".

1405
"No innkeeper (hospes), wineseller, brewster or female seller ('Vendatrix') called tippler shall permit any inhabitants or strangers to reside or remain by night in their taverns after nine o'clock has struck in the night except true and honest persons for whose doings their hosts will answer to the lord the King and the community of the town."
(*Report of the Manuscripts page 57*)

1458
"The said innkeepers shall not bake or cause to be baked in any way any horse-bread, but shall buy it from the common bakers aforesaid and of no one else ... the common bakers shall yearly for ever serve the said innkeepers with such horse-bread good and sufficient viz. fifteen to the dozen as often as required by the said innkeepers."
(*Report on the manuscripts page 87/88*)

1557
Thirty-eight brewsters listed in Beverley.
(*Report on the Manuscripts page 180*)

1558
"Nine persons fined 2s each for selling beer contrary to the ordinance."
(*Report on the Manuscripts page 181*)

1573
"Sixty-two fined for brewing without licence."
(*Report on the Manuscripts page 183*)

1574
"Forty-five brewsters fined for selling ale with unlawful measures."
(*Report on the Manuscripts page 183*)

1592
"Every person hereafter licensed to keep an alehouse, typling house, inn or taverne shall pay yearly to the town 20s. The mayor and justices shall not admit above forty-five alehouses etc. to be kept within the town. The persons to be of honest fame credit and behaviour and to be bound with sureties to pay the yearly payment."
(*Beverley Borough Records page 97*)

1592
"It was ordered in 1592 that no more than forty alehouses should be allowed in the town. Several are known by name like the Bull outside North bar, the Swan within the bar, the Hart in Wednesday Market, and the Tabard in Eastgate."
(*VCH page 87*)

1596
"Every inhabitant of the town who shall at any time resort, use, or frequent any "alehouse or typling house inn or taverne (except for some urgent cause or for the benefit of the town...and remain more than two hours in any day) or in any place shall be drunk or otherwise misbehave himself in

word or deed. Forfeit 12s and for misbehaviour 40s."
(*Beverley Borough Records page 38*)

17th Century

"The inns included the George and the Talbot in Highgate, the White Horse, and the Bell."
(*VCH page 110*)

1686

"In 1686 it was reported that there were one hundred and eighty two guest beds in Beverley and stabling for four hundred and sixty horses."
(*VCH page 110*)

1671

A coin or check exists with the legend "Wm. Johnson at the Coffee House in Beverley" dated 1671.

18th Century

"Notable among those meeting places were two inns in North Bar Within, the Blue Bell, renamed the Beverley Arms after rebuilding was completed in 1796, and the Tiger. When the Blue Bell was offered to let in 1752 it was said that "at the said inn the justices of the peace for the riding at the two general quarter sessions in every year, the commissioners of the sewers, and likewise the commissioners of the land tax and window money meet there, and the excise office is there". The two inns were also the meeting places of the enclosure commissioners and turnpike trustees, and it was there that the gentlemen and clergy of the riding considered topics as diverse as the preservation of game and Roman Catholic emancipation. From the 1760s both inns also entertained the East Riding Agricultural Society and the Tiger was the meeting place of a freemasons' lodge

established in 1793 and of a hunt club formed in 1808."
(*VCH page 112*)

"The facilities of the Blue Bell included a Bowling Green in 1752 and a subscription coffee room by 1793."
(*VCH page 113*)

"As the number of maltsters declined (twenty-eight between 1715 and 1734, nine in 1774 and only three in 1830...) that of brewers increased, from one in 1774 to six in 1830 and the larger businesses combined malting and brewing. Among the brewers was Robert Stephenson who bought the Golden Ball and its brewery in Toll Gavel in 1797. Earlier brewing had been carried on in inns and alehouses of which there were 48 in 1725."
(*VCH page 115*)

1715-1734

Sixty-four innkeepers.
(*VCH page 114*)

1725

Forty-eight inns and alehouses.
(*VCH page 115*)

1756

"There were reported to be two hundred and twenty-two guest beds in the town in 1756, with stabling for three hundred and sixty-one horses."
(*VCH page 115*)

1774

Twenty-seven innkeepers.
(*VCH page 104*)

1830
Twenty-five innkeepers in 1830.
(*VCH page 115*)

1834
"Fifty drinking places including thirteen beer houses."
(*VCH page 115*)

1839
"Beverley's Total Abstinence Society formed" (*Jan Crowther*)
[One Temperance Hall of circa 1846 still survives in Well Lane. (*Chris Ketchell*)]

1908
The annual Beverley Licensing Sessions for the year ended 31st December 1908 noted:

Public houses, including spirit merchants and railway refreshment rooms...................................42
Beer-houses (on)..12
Total public and beer-houses....................54
Shops selling beer (off)............................3
Shops selling wine (on)..............................1
Shops selling wine (off)............................3
Shops selling wine and spirits (off)............2
Total licenses of all kinds................. 63

"The proportion is one public-house or beer-house to every 244 inhabitants"
"For drunkenness etc.; proceedings were taken against 79 males and 34 females, total of 113, of whom 5 were discharged, 53 committed to prison, 53 fined and 2 ordered to find sureties. Forty-two of these persons were known to have been previously convicted, one a non-resident, over 80 times".

1912
Public houses with a full licence..................36
Public houses with a 6 day licence
& early closing 2
Public houses with a 6 day licence.................1
Beer houses (on)..10
Beer houses (off)...3
Beer houses with a 6 day licence..................1
Sweets and wine (off)..1
Wine (off)..3
Wine & spirits (off)...1
Total licenses of all kinds............................58

The population according to the 1911 census was 13,654. This meant that there was one public house or beer house for every 273 inhabitants.

1988
The population of Beverley in 1988 was approximately 21,000, which meant that there was one pub for every 583 inhabitants.

2000
In the year 2000 there were thirty-eight pubs in Beverley and the population was still approximately 21,000, which suggests one pub for every 552 inhabitants.

2001
In the year 2001 nineteen of Beverley's pubs are Grade II listed buildings, three of which are Grade II *star* listed. Of its surviving buildings that were previously pubs – another thirteen are Grade II listed, one of those also Grade II *star* listed.

Bibliography

Be Your Own House Detective. David Austin, Mac Dowdy, Judith Miller. BBC Books. London, 1997.

Beverley Borough Records 1575-1821. Yorkshire Archaeological Society Series LXXXIV. Edited by J. Dennett, 1933.

Beverley Guardian Newspaper. Various editions - mostly 19th Century.

Beverley in Mid-Victorian Times. Jan Crowther. Hutton Press Ltd. Beverley, 1990.

Beverley Minute Books 1707-1835. Yorkshire Archaeological Society Series CXXI. Edited by K. A. Macmahon, 1958.

Beverley Poll Books. 1784, 1806, 1837, and 1868. (Beverley Local Studies Library).

Beverley's Pubs. Christopher Ketchell. Hull College Local History Unit. Hull, 1998.

Brewer's Dictionary of Phrase & Fable (Millenium Edition). Revised by Adrian Broom. Cassel & Co. London, 2001.

Britain in Old Photographs; Around Beverley. Patricia E. Deans and John Markham. Alan Sutton Publishing. Stroud, 1995.

British Inn Signs and their Stories. Eric R Delderfield. David & Charles. Newton Abbot, 1965.

Doorways into Beverley's past. Berna Moody. Highgate Publications (Beverley) Ltd., 1991.

East Riding of the County of York, Minutes of the Proceedings of the County Licensing Committee 1904-1923. Wright & Hoggard. Minster Press. Beverley, 1924.

East Riding of the County of York, Minutes of the Proceedings of the County Licensing Committee 1924-1934. Wright & Hoggard. Minster Press. Beverley, 1934.

East Riding Friendly Societies. David Neave. East Yorkshire Local History Society. Beverley, 1988.

English Place-Name Society. Volume XIV, the Place Names of the East Riding of Yorkshire. A.H. Smith. Cambridge University Press, 1937.

Hengate, Ladygate, Walkergate 1981. Ivan & Elizabeth Hall, o.b.o. Beverley Friary Preservation Trust. Notes on houses open to the public in 1981.

Highgate 1977. Beverley Friary Preservation Trust. Notes on houses open to the public in 1977.

Historic Beverley. Ivan and Elizabeth Hall. William Sessions Ltd. York, 1973.

Hull and East Yorkshire Breweries: From the Eighteenth Century to the Present. Pat Aldabella and Robert Barnard. East Yorkshire Local History Society. 1997.

Hull University Manuscripts and Archives Database, www.hull.ac.uk/lib/archives/humad2

Illustrated Handbook to Beverley. J.J. Sheahan. Green & Son. Beverley, 1903.

Keldgate & Minster Moorgate. Beverley Friary Preservation Trust. Notes on houses open to the public in 1979.

Moors' & Robson's Breweries Ltd., A Brief History. Robert Barnard. Hull College Local History Unit. Hull, 1996.

Old Beverley. Philip Brown. East Yorkshire Local History Society in Association with Humberside Leisure Services. Beverley, 1983.

Report on the Manuscripts of the Corporation of Beverley. Historical Manuscripts Commission. HMSO, 1900.

Royal Commission on Historical Monuments Supplementary Series: 4. Beverley, An Archaeological and Architectural Study. Keith Miller, John Robinson, Barbara English and Ivan Hall. H.M.S.O. London, 1982.

Some Past History of Beverley (*George Armstrong's Diaries*). Unpublished facsimile of the hand-written reminiscences of an *old Beverley butcher* circa 1896-1920. Beverley Local Studies Library (Y/942.74/BEV. B263756993.)

Tales of Old Inns, Richard Keverne (Revised and ed. by Hammond Innes 1947). Collins. London, 1939.

Telephone Directory, Hull & District. Various editions.

The Announcer Newspaper. Various editions - mostly 1930s.

The Beverley Arms, the Story of a Hotel. John Markham. Highgate Publications (Beverley) Ltd., 1986.

The Buildings of England, Yorkshire: York and the East Riding. Nikolaus Pevsner and David Neave. Penguin Books. London, 1972 (Revised edition of 1995).

The Development of the Streets of Beverley (Index Edition). David Sherwood. Hull College Local History Unit. Hull, 1996.

The English Inn Past & Present (A Review of its History & Social Life), A E Richardson & H D Eberlein. B T Batsford Ltd. London, 1925.

The Inn Places of Beverley. Frank Pinfold and George Higginson. Hutton Press. Beverley, 1988.

The Lost Streets of Beverley. David Sherwood. Hull College Local History Unit. Hull, 1997.

The Old Tiger Inn, Beverley; the Story of a Georgian Coaching Inn. John Markham. Highgate Publications (Beverley) Ltd. 1988.

The Oxford Companion to Local and Family History. David Hey (ed.) Oxford University Press. 1996.

The Signboards of Beverley. *"The Rambler, an old-time Scribe"*, articles from The Announcer newspaper. January to February 1939, Beverley.

The Timber Framed House in England. Trudy West, Newton Abbott, 1971.

The Victoria History of the County of York, East Riding Volume VI: The Borough and Liberties of Beverley. Edited by K.J. Allison. Oxford University Press, 1989.

Trade Directories: Battle's 1791, 1814/15. Baines' 1822, 1823, 1826. White's 1826, 1831. Pigot's 1834. White's 1840, 1846. Slater's 1848. White's 1851. Slater's 1855. Melville's 1855. White's 1858, 1859. Slater's 1864. White's 1867. Kelly's 1872, 1879. White's 1882. Slater's 1887. Kelly's 1889, 1893, 1897. Cook's 1899, 1901. Kelly's 1901, 1905, 1906, 1907, 1908, 1909, 1910, 1912, 1913, 1915, 1916, 1919, 1920, 1921, 1922, 1925, 1926, 1929, 1930, 1933, 1937, 1939.

Two Recently Demolished Beverley Buildings. David Neave. An article in the Beverley Civic Society Newsletter circa 1970.

Ward's Family Almanac (1861-1916). John Ward. Beverley. (Beverley Local Studies Library).

Maps and plans

All the location maps and plans in this work have been drawn by the author, and are mostly based on Ordnance Survey plans compiled from the surveys made in 1852-53 and 1890-91. The maps are of no fixed date and are for illustration only. The pubs illustrated did not necessarily exist concurrently with others shown on the same map.

The majority of the building plans are held at the East Riding of Yorkshire Council Archive Office in Beverley, mostly archived at BOBE/6. The full list of plans consulted is as follows:

BOBE/6/1873-7 "Alterations to the Oddfellows Arms"
BOBE/6/1874-23 "Two cottages and a tavern in Cherry Tree Lane"
BOBE/6/1875-64 "Alterations to the Reindeer Inn"
BOBE/6/1875-65 "New dram shop window at Royal Standard"
BOBE/6/1876-83 "Alterations at the Beehive Inn"
BOBE/6/1878-146 "Alterations at the Buck Inn"
BOBE/6/1885-152 "Alterations to the spirit vaults in Ladygate"
BOBE/6/1888-211 "Alterations at the Red Lion"
BOBE/6/1895-1 "Additions to the George & Dragon Inn"
BOBE/6/1896-21 "Alterations to the Traveller's Rest"
BOBE/6/1899-2 "New public house and shop at 30 Toll Gavel"
BOBE/6/1901-26 "Alterations to the Royal Oak"
BOBE/6/1902-13 "Alterations to the Malt Shovel"
BOBE/6/1902-20 "Alterations to the George Inn"
BOBE/6/1902-23 "Alterations to the Moulders Arms"
BOBE/6/1905-9 "Alterations to the Sun Inn"
BOBE/6/1906-13 "Alterations to the Sloop Inn"
BOBE/6/1907-8 "New public house in Holme Church Lane"
BOBE/6/1908-20 "Alterations to the Green Dragon"
BOBE/6/1909-19 "Urinal & Privvies at the Gate Inn"
BOBE/6/1912-8 "Additions to 13 Flemingate"
BOBE/6/1912-10 "Alterations to the Tiger Inn"
BOBE/6/1912-17 "Alterations to the Windmill Inn"
BOBE/6/1913-2 "New doorway for the Beaver Hotel"
BOBE/6/1914-19 "Alterations to the Oddfellows Inn"

BOBE/6/1919-6 "Alterations to the Mariners Arms"
BOBE/6/1921-8 "Alterations to the Buck Inn"
BOBE/6/1922-4 "Alterations to the Kings Head"
BOBE/6/1925-5 "Improvements to the Globe Inn"
BOBE/6/1925-25 "Sanitary improvements at the Cattle Market Tavern"
BOBE/6/1926-2 "Alterations to the Queens Head"
BOBE/6/1927-7 "Alterations to the Old White Swan"
BOBE/6/1927-18 "Alterations to the Valiant Soldier"
BOBE/6/1927-42 "Alterations to the Tanners Arms"
BOBE/6/1929-9a "New public house - Dog & Duck"
BOBE/6/1930-30 "Alterations to the Rose & Crown"
BOBE/6/1930-40a "Alterations to the Tiger Inn"
BOBE/6/1930-45 "Alterations to the Tiger Inn"
BOBE/6/1931-9 "New shopfront to the Old Holderness Hotel"
BOBE/6/1936-23 "Alterations to the Durham Ox"
BOBE/6/1936-28 "Rebuilding of Lady Le Gros"
BOBE/6/1936-29 "Alterations at the Moulders Arms"
BOBE/6/1937-3 "Alterations at the Foresters Arms"
BOBE/6/1937-28 "Alterations and additions at the Mariners Arms"
BOBE/6/1938-7 "Alterations and additions at the Sloop Inn"
BOBE/6/1938-14 "Alterations at the Green Dragon"
BOBE/6/1938-27 "New Inn, rebuilding the Foresters Arms"
BOBE/6/1952-782 "Internal alterations at the Malt Shovel"
BOBE/6/1954-964 "Rebuilding the Beehive Inn"

Other image sources

To include every available picture that I have found during my research for the book would have been prohibitive in terms of cost. The reader may wish to look at some of the other images of the pubs; those available for easy reference are as follows:

Admiral Duncan/Hallgarth Inn: See drawing by Luke Clennell c1835-40 in Old Beverley page 6.

Arden's Vaults: Interior on page 41 of Historic Beverley.

Beaver: Beverley Library Post Card No.1439 circa 1910, and PC No.1035 (image circa 1861).

Beverley Arms: Engraving in Beverley Art Gallery circa 1780 by Thomas Malton Junior (also reproduced in Old Beverley page 23).

Black Swan: Beverley Library PC No.835 circa 1905.

Cross Keys: Beverley Library has at least one picture in its "Old Beverley file".

Globe Inn: Beverley Library has pictures of the front and rear in its "Old Beverley file" and some in the "Calvert Collection" file No.5.

Green Dragon: Beverley Library has one picture in its "Old Beverley file". See also - Old Beverley pages 28, 29 and 30.

Holderness Hotel: See Humberside Libraries postcard reprint No.13 of Toll Gavel circa 1905, which shows the pub on the right.

Kings Head: Beverley Library has one picture in its "Old Beverley file".

Lord Nelson: Beverley Library has PC No.1825 circa 1905 and one picture in its "Old Beverley file".

Malt Shovel: Beverley Library has PC No.815.

Nag's Head: See picture in "Around Beverley" page 71, which shows a part of the building.

Pack Horse: Old Beverley page 29 shows the Pack Horse.

Push Inn: See Old Beverley page 30; Around Beverley page 31 & 32; and Historic Beverley fig.202 on page 84 shows the later Georgian shop fronts.

Queen's Head: See page 18 of Britain in Old Photographs – Around Beverley, and image No.32 in Old Beverley.

Railway Inn: Beverley Library has PC No.1073.

Spotted Cow: Image No.37 in Old Beverley shows a drawing of the original frontage circa 1845.

Sun Inn: Beverley Library has PC No.1193 circa 1905 and one in its "Old Beverley" file.

Also see wrongly captioned water-colour by Luke Clennell, (circa 1835) in Beverley In Mid-Victorian Times page 51, which is probably the oldest illustration of the Sun Inn (the junction of Flemingate and Eastgate has been confused more than once; the 1826 directory also listed the Sun's address as Eastgate).

Tiger Inn: See illustration by Luke Clennell c1835-40 in Old Beverley page 40.

Valiant Soldier: Beverley Library has one picture in its "Old Beverley file".

White Swan: See photo in Old Beverley page 30.

Index

Windmill Walk. 112
Wood Lane. 18, 20, 21, 33
Woolpack Inn, Westwood Road. 113, 114
Worlds End, Keldgate. 114

York Road. 84, 85, 86

LOST PUBS OF HULL

Paul Gibson and Graham Wilkinson

A unique insight into Hull's social life is revealed in this pictorial reminder of the variety of types and styles of pub which featured as part of the city's landscape.

Lost Pubs of Hull, containing more than 100 photographs, many published for the first time and each thoroughly researched, is a tribute to many of the city's fondly remembered institutions, as well as a nostalgic step back in time.

Price £12.75

ISBN 1 902039 03 3

Kingston Press

www.hullcc.gov.uk/kingstonpress

Sales City Information Service, Hull Central Library, Albion Street, Kingston upon Hull HU1 3TF

Telephone: (01482) 223344
Fax: (01482) 616896
E-mail: city.information@hullcc.gov.uk
and all good bookshops